George W. Owen

The Leech Club

Or, The Mysteries of the Catskills

George W. Owen

The Leech Club
Or, The Mysteries of the Catskills

ISBN/EAN: 9783743306004

Manufactured in Europe, USA, Canada, Australia, Japa

Cover: Foto ©ninafisch / pixelio.de

Manufactured and distributed by brebook publishing software (www.brebook.com)

George W. Owen

The Leech Club

OR, THE

MYSTERIES OF THE CATSKILLS.

BY

GEORGE W. OWEN.

———◆◆◆———

BOSTON:
LEE & SHEPARD, PUBLISHERS.
NEW YORK:
LEE, SHEPARD & DILLINGHAM.
1874.

Entered according to Act of Congress, in the year 1874, by
GEORGE W. OWEN,
In the Office of the Librarian of Congress, at Washington, D. C.

THE LEECH CLUB;

OR,

THE MISTERIES OF THE CATSKILLS.

CHAPTER I.

ABOVE THE CLOUDS.

It matters not about the precise date of this tale. The events herein narrated are of such recent occurrence that most of the characters are still living, and should the dates be too nicely fixed, many who figure in these pages would be pestered with inquiries from the curious that might not be pleasant.

One who will readily be recognized as a principal character of this narrative, as it develops itself, will here be introduced. Not in a richly-furnished parlor, nor in a counting-room with the concomitants of commercial wealth; nor yet in a lowly tenement or cottage, or an unpretending place of business; nor in a palace coach, or second-class railway car; nor jauntily dashing along upon the highway behind a spirited team of chargers; nor yet trudging wearily through lanes, by-ways or frequented avenues, an object of commiseration to the more wealthy traveler sailing by with his elegant turnout. We must introduce our hero, the better to set forth his true character, where there were no thoroughfares or beaten paths; where the world could scarcely be cognizant of his existence, and where he, if he looked down upon the world at all, only did so to regret that *it* existed, and that his walking dream of ethereal bliss was not a reality.

The Catskills! The name suggests to the whilom voyager on the classic Hudson a vision of airy and weird peaks, and recollections of mysterious legends. Stretching for miles parallel with the upper Hudson, from six to twelve miles from the river, a valley intervening, variegated with farms, woodlands, glens, winding rivulets sparkling through deep ravines, forest-capped hills,—those grand old mountains in the rear present to the enchanted gaze of the traveler the forms of collossal deities, with a mosaic-carpeted amphitheater in front, where admiring pilgrims may come and worship at their feet.

Not many years ago, had a voyager on the deck of a passing Hudson steamer been provided with a powerful telescope, and happened to direct it to a certain one of the high peaks of the Catskills, he would have observed a man treading its airy heights, alone, or at least with no companions but his own thoughts, the fleeting clouds, the shapeless rocks, and the varied objects of nature that were evidently engrossing his attention. It was just such a day as the admirer of mountain scenery would choose for the ascension of a high peak. It was not perfectly clear, nor yet so cloudy but an outlook upon the grand panorama around could generally be obtained through the rifts which the stiff breeze was constantly making in the hurrying clouds.

There he strode as one walking on ethereal heights, having abandoned the world below as too earthly for the engrossment of immortal mind. The rugged peaks of the Catskills were spread out around him like a sea of immense billows, which had been petrified into solid masses in some long past geological age; while now from their sides spring forests of deep, rich foliage, separated into terraces by massive and perpendicular ledges of rock, with almost the regularity of human art, and with the grandeur only reached by the master hand of Nature. The billowy peaks are separated by immense ravines, through which tumble streams of water in continuous cataracts, anon receiving accessions from the mountain sides; as if the upheaval of this sea of rocks were again melting into its original liquid, and giving it back to the yawning gorges. In just such magnificent confusion as might be expected to arise from a greatly agitated sea, lie the detached *debris* of rocks, which have apparently been caps or fragments of billows broken off from the more gigantic waves, and incontinently petrified. Some immense boulders stand upon the end; as if the Titans of old had engaged in the amusement of balancing pyramids upon the apex. Sometimes two gigantic slabs will meet each other at the top at an inclination; suggesting the thought that some giant aborigine had made his wigwam by hurling two rocks together. Sometimes a nicely chiseled passage will be found cut through a ledge; furnishing for antiquarians a possible theory that the pre-Adamite inhabitants of the country had made cuts through the solid rock for some thoroughfare older than the Appian way. Openings frequently appear in the solid rock, forming rooms sometimes shapeless as the den of a wild beast, but often of regular dimensions, having the angles clearly defined; where, perhaps, some feudal Titan had chiseled out in the hard rock under his castle a gloomy prison for such of his vassals as might incur his displeasure.

The flying clouds played around these wild peaks like charging battalions of the warring elements, while the individual we have mentioned, walked upon the mountain crests, apparently communing with the objects of grandeur around. None of the pigmy affairs of the lower world seemed worthy of his attention. He spoke to the mountain, and the opening gorge was the mouth from which came the answer. If he felt human at all, it was as one standing upon the very pinnacles of earthly affairs, where the terrestrial and ethereal meet; where man feels that he has glimpses into the arcana of the celestial, and anticipates a little of the experience which he can only fully realize by mounting entirely beyond the influence of sublunary things. The rifts in the clouds revealed to him the cultivated world below, and occasionally reminded him that he was human; while the inexpressible coloring imparted by the sun to the massive, irregular clouds, which appeared almost blended with the jagged mountain peaks, caused the openings, with the blue sky beyond, to appear like celestial gates, through which he, favored of mortals, had the momentary pleasure of gazing. Thus he almost imagined himself as walking on clouds; as holding converse with the forces of nature; as grasping both the ethereal and the terrestrial; which seemed, for the moment, a state of even greater bliss than that enjoyed by the happy spirits of the departed.

Such are the inspirations presented to him who truly appreciates mountain scenery.

CHAPTER II.

LOOKING DOWN UPON A THUNDER-STORM.

The lower legions of clouds, wearied with the aimless marching and counter-marching through empty space, finally began to marshal their forces into a solid mass, evidently intent upon some enterprise of moment. It appeared as if the standard which these misty battalions all recognized, had been reared by some commanding cloud; and directly there was a rushing for the common rallying point. The skirmishing mists were called in; the light troops which had been apparently acting as flying *vedettes*, came galloping toward the rendezvous; the more massive bodies of clouds, like outlying divisions of an army, moved with a slower, firmer, but not less surer tread toward the position where the forces were gathering.

Soon the individual we have observed upon one of the lofty peaks, found the peak on which he stood, environed by a solid mass of black, angry clouds. But this mass was several hundred feet below him. Above and all around the point where he stood was a cloudless sky. Apparently the clouds which had a short time before been flying through space overhead, and all around, had gathered in the grand rally just beneath the feet of our hero. The sun, which had reached a point about half way between the meridian and the horizon, shone forth with all the splendor of noonday upon the peak where he stood, and upon the dark mass of clouds beneath.

The view of the lower world was entirely shut off with the exception of a gap in the vast body of dark clouds. This divided the body much like two contending armies.

And now the battle of the elements commenced. The guns were unlimbered, and the thundering artillery rolled in deafening reverberations through the gorges, ravines and caverns of the mountains. The forked lightning darted across the chasm which separated the two masses of clouds, making them verily appear like two battling armies hurling at each other their fiery thunderbolts. Occasionally would be heard an astounding roar, as if all the batteries in both armies had opened at once, or as if a gigantic mine had been exploded, and a huge mountain had been blown to atoms. In addition to the thundering explosions, there was heard a constant roar, as of the fierce breathing of many winds, and the mighty rushing of many waters. The upper face of the dark mass of clouds, as the spectator looked down upon it, presented the surface of a troubled sea, whose billows were splendidly and variously colored and shaded by the bright sunlight; while anon terrific explosions would resound from its uttermost depths; and tortuous streaks of lightning would dart over the surface like fiery sea-serpents chasing their prey.

If the spectator who stood above, contemplating this scene of awful grandeur, had before been constrained to consider himself lifted above the earth in standing upon those peaks, he could, with a very little additional stretch of the imagination, have fancied himself a demigod directing the battle of the elements below; if, indeed, he could so far forget human littleness as to conceive it capable of commanding such supernatural forces. The position was one either to humiliate or elevate the beholder. If he viewed it in terror, he could not otherwise than be humbled into the dust. If he embraced the scene as an immortal spirit which had been favored with a view of the eternal, such as is deigned to few that have not escaped the clog of clay which obscures the vision of the soul, then he must have been elated beyond expression, and viewed the scene as an exhibition of the power of which he himself was a component part—assuming the truth of the doctrine that man is a spark from his Maker. View it as he would, the scene was one never to be forgotten.

But our hero was soon to be startled from his contemplative mood, and brought to a sense of the realities of his situation. The storm did not long confine itself to the regions below the mountain peak where he stood. Gradually arising, the clouds soon enveloped the peak, and soon he was drenched in the driving rain. No shelter was at hand, and amid the blinding storm he commenced descending the peak toward the west.

The formation of the Catskill mountains is not peculiarly favorable to a rapid and safe descent down their sides by a pedestrian. The mountain side is often composed of a succession of terraces, each terrace bounded by a high, rocky precipice. Thus the traveler, as he attempts to descend the mountain, soon finds himself hemmed off by a precipice, that stops his progress. He finds that he is upon a narrow, natural terrace which he has no alternative but to follow until he finds a break in the rocky wall. By clambering down among boulders, catching to trees, shrubs and crags, he manages to descend to the next terrace, again to find his further progress in that direction barred by another precipice. He is simply on another terrace, along which he must carefully thread his way, till he comes to another break in the wall. How long it will take him to descend the mountain in this manner depends either on his good fortune in striking broken sections in the terrace wall, or his knowledge of the locality of the same.

Our hero was not acquainted with the mountains. He was soon lost in the labyrinth of terraces, and wandered about at random. The blinding rain continued to descend in torrents, darkness set in, and the situation became alarming. The hideous roar of the thunder re-echoing from a thousand gorges and ravines, the lurid flashes of lightning, momentarily lighting up the weird rocks, caverns and gnarled trees, would have overwhelmed a less resolute heart. He had need to tread with the utmost caution, else he would have been dashed to atoms down some awful precipice. The glaring lightning was an agent of good, for it served to light his dubious and dangerous path. With calm fortitude he pursued his aimless way; the lightning like an ignis fatuus luring him on; hopeful that he would finally extricate himself from the trying situation.

SUPERNATURAL APPEARANCES.

The terrors which beset him were not confined to the belching thunder, or the danger of being hurled from a precipice. Strange noises filled the intervals between the rolling thunder and its echoes. Whisperings filled the air; figures which seemed to be a compromise between substance and the impalpable air, brushed past him, their insubstantial garments making the slightest abrasion against his own apparel. He approached a narrow, rocky defile, through which he must pass. As he neared it, a continuous glare of sheet lightning illuminated the gorge. There appeared, seated on the rocks on either side of the defile, a number of figures, half man, half demon. Almost paralyzed with astonishment, he stopped short, debating in his mind whether to recede or advance. The glare of lightning continued in the most unaccountable manner, revealing to his vision the figures in a way that seemed conclusive that he could not be mistaken. Frantic with desperation, he hurled his walking stick at one of the figures, only a few feet off. It seemed to pass through the object with no more impression than on empty space. Presently the glare of lightning subsided, and nothing was to be seen. Accusing himself of foolishly imagining the presence of ghostly beings, he rushed forward; but just as he had gotten fully within the gorge, a similar, continuous glare of lightning again revealed his ghostly neighbors; this time so near that he could have touched them with his hand. As he rushed forward through this demoniacal gauntlet, a hollow laugh saluted his ears; and he was only too glad that this was drowned by a rolling explosion of thunder.

How far he wandered among the nightly terrors of the Catskills, it is impossible to say. It was near midnight when the storm ceased, the sky became clear, and the moon shone down faintly through the openings in the foliage of the giant trees. Threading his way on through the mountains, he finally saw lights twinkling through the trees. Approaching, he came to a brawling stream of water. The volume of water and swift running current rendered the stream unfordable, and he followed it down till he came in sight of a building. A short distance from the edifice the stream parted into two currents, commingling again below the building, and falling in a beautiful cascade into a small lake. The building was thus located on an island, and as the volume of water in the two streams was considerable, and the current swift, the house could only be reached by means of a bridge.

It was now about midnight, and after the terrific ordeal through which our hero had passed, it was with some trepidation that he approached this moated dwelling, which appeared like a castle in the wilderness. The bridge was evidently constructed as a draw, but it was at that time in the proper position for crossing. He felt as if entering upon enchanted ground as he crossed the threshold of the lonely precincts. Had he been superstitious, he never would have approached this dubious looking dwelling after the experiences of that night. It is true he did not feel certain that he might not meet just such strange beings as had haunted his fearful wanderings in the mountains. After a brief survey of the premises, he came to the conclusion that the constructors of this building must have something more than ghostly attributes, and chilled with the rain and exhausted by his wanderings, he determined to see if the inmates possessed human hospitalities. Drawing near to the building he heard music, and this rather reassured him; for he reasoned that evil spirits do not cultivate such refining arts, and that men who do so, must have considerable humanity still left in them.

Approaching the door, he raised a huge knocker, which descending on the plate, caused the mountain dells around to echo, and called forth growls and barking from several unseen dogs about the premises. He was admitted. And what was his astonishment to be ushered into a spacious, finely-furnished room, and a large company of gaily-dressed ladies and gentlemen! At one end of the room was stationed a band of musicians, while several sets of dancers were on the floor, either having been engaged in a quadrille, or just about to commence one. The entrance of the stranger brought matters to a halt, and all gathered around to view this visitor from the outward realms of night. Our hero's clothes were dripping with wet, and his countenance wore an anxious, but not terrified expression. Some brief questions followed; to which he answered that he had accidentally gotten lost in the mountains. He was puzzled beyond expression at finding such a dwelling and such a company there; but restraining his curiosity, he was conducted to a room where a wood fire was speedily started in a fireplace. Refreshments were placed before him; after partaking of which, and drying himself by the fire, he was shown to a sleeping apartment. Having thus disposed of our hero, after a troublous night, such as seldom falls to the lot of mortals, we will return to the company in the large parlor.

The dancers had seemingly given up their festivities, and were gathered in groups discussing the apparition of the stranger at such an unseasonable hour. By observing their conversation we may gather something respecting their quality, and the cause of their being assembled in this singular locality. The appearance of the company, viewed in comparison with the surrounding concomitants, was enough to excite the amazement, if not superstition, of any one who had not forgotten the fairy tales of the nursery, learned in childhood. Amid the surrounding poverty of rocks, forests and mountain gorges, whence those costly toilets, those sparkling diamonds, glittering jewelry, and rich attire of every description? The rooms, too, were furnished with a gorgeousness that immeasurably belied the situation. The parlors of no merchant prince in the distant city could outdo those of this forest palace in superfluous richness.

Were the house and furniture a solid reality, and the festive throng, persons of real flesh and blood? or were the building and its garniture but the conjuration of the ruling genius of the mountains, and the gaily-bedecked semblances of men and women, the airy genii, who had so greatly frightened our hero in his nightly meanderings, and now gathered in a fairy palace to entertain, after having so sorely persecuted him? Such freaks are not inconsistent with the genii of the story books. But, having exhausted all conjectures without arriving at any conclusion, we will listen to the conversation of the genii, and see if we can gather anything more tangible from that. First speaks a gorgeous looking fairy, who might have been taken for Titania, the queen of her tribe:

"Isn't it curious! I do believe that strange man has been rained down in the shower, or shot from the clouds in one of those awful claps of thunder!"

"Yes, indeed, Mrs. Grandola,"—answered a masculine genius arrayed in immense gorgeousness, suggestive of the idea that he might be Oberon, king of the fairies,—" yes, indeed, Mrs. Grandola, the stranger looked as scared as if he had either fallen from a cloud or been interviewed by some of those goblins of the Catskills that we hear so much about."

"Nonsense, Mr. Swellup! I don't believe one word of these idle stories."

"But," struck in a spruce little masculine fairy, who might have been Puck, "if you should have such ocular demonstration as I had in these mountains one night, I warrant you would change your opinion."

"Poh! Mr. Flitaway, ever since you were before that investigating committee in regard to that little matter of a hundred thousand which your bill for stationery is said to have been 'raised,' you have been haunted by accusing ghosts."

"I think, now, Mrs. Grandola," said a young man with diamond rings and enormous fob, "you have hit the nail on the head. I should not be surprised if this scared looking stranger is an agent of one of those pestiferous investigating committees, sent here to spy out our Club House, and gather what information he can, to be used against us by our persecutors."

"If I thought he was," said another, "I would give him to the pet wolf out there in the cage for a collation."

"Isn't it a burning shame," said a young lady, loaded with jewelry, and so encumbered with trailing laces that what little humanity was visible, appeared rather like an ornamented wax figure accidentally dropped into a confused mass of rich dry goods,—" isn't it a burning shame that people cannot enjoy the elegancies of life purchased by their own money without being hunted by these hounds, who are only jealous because they have not the means to live in as good style as some of their neighbors!"

"Ah! Miss Gossamer," said a young fellow in a bantering tone, "there is a difference of opinion as to the ownership of the fine things you speak of. A good many are of the opinion that a thousand yards or so of that variety store you carry about with you, belong to the tax-payers."

"And," retorted Miss Gossamer, "how much would be left of you, your fob-chains, diamond rings and exquisite tailoring, if the tax payers had their dues?"

"Tut, tut!" broke in Mr. Swellup, "remember the old proverb, 'when certain persons fall out among themselves, certain other persons get their dues'; in which case we might all lose what we possess."

"Indeed, Mr. Swellup," said Mrs. Grandola, "you speak just as if there was truth in the hue and cry that is made about our getting our money wrongfully from the public funds."

"Oh! no, Mrs. Grandola, I was only talking from the standpoint assumed by this young lady and gentleman."

"And I," said the young gentleman alluded to, "was only giving Miss Gossamer a delicate compliment on her magnificent toilet."

"And I," said Miss Gossamer, "only intended to show my friend that I appreciated a compliment coming from so profound a source."

The conversation continued in a similar strain for a considerable time, when this unique assemblage began to drop away by ones and twos. Whatever opinion the reader may have formed in regard to the supernatural appearances which our hero encountered in his nocturnal wanderings, he has doubtless ere this come to the conclusion that the inhabitants of this strange dwelling were not of a ghostly nature; and that when they left the brilliant parlors, they did not disappear through solid walls of rock or inconceivably narrow crevices into the caves of the mountains;

nor flit away in volatile bodies into the air, and take up their residences on shining clouds to catch the first brilliant rays of the orb of day as he imparts the glorious tints to the clouds and mountain peaks. Not they, indeed. They were rather of the earth, earthy, and when they left the banqueting halls, it was only to retire to their sleeping apartments in the castellated building, that they might acquire new strength to pursue their festive rounds, and consume the substance of the land; on which they feed like a school of leeches.

CHAPTER III.

HORACE LACKFATHE.

WE must leave our hero to his dreams or meditations in the strange domicile, and go to his native place, and see what we can learn of his history. Horace Lackfathe, whom we have followed through a night of wild adventure into what must have appeared to him as the castle of demons or fairies, was born in a small village in a neighboring State. Though born poor, he had managed, by his own exertions, to obtain a good education. He had developed talent of no ordinary degree, and having chosen the legal profession, bid fair to arise to eminence. He had already obtained considerable distinction in his own town, was valued and even courted by the community as a rising young man of high moral principle. He, for a time, felt flattered and gratified at the consideration and success he had achieved, and was stimulated thereby to exertion to rise still higher in the estimation of his fellow-men. Many had already predicted that he one day would occupy high places in private or official life.

But after a few years there was, if not a falling off, at least a stay of progress on the part of Horace Lackfathe. He did not advance to that position which had been predicted for him. He seemed, after having reached a certain point, to be content with mediocrity. Not that his talents or abilities had been overrated. There was in him the germ of greatness; but for some reason he failed, neglected, or did not care to develop it. He did not depreciate in the respect of his fellow-citizens, for he was a man of high moral tone. He only disappointed those who knew how great a mind he possessed.

The trouble was, Horace Lackfathe had formed in his own mind too high a standard of the excellence of mankind. He had conceived the average human being to be actuated chiefly by principles of honor and magnanimity. Selfishness, moral obliquity, and unscrupulousness in adapting the means to the end, were the exceptions in the Utopian world in which he lived. A natural and intuitive disposition to live uprightly, and deal guilelessly, was the attribute of the man of his conception. He did not believe that a considerable portion of the business world were a set of over-reaching tricksters, who consider it the height of business acumen to get the best of their neighbors in a sharp bargain; he did not believe that the average practitioners in his own profession thought it the refinement of legal *finesse* to carry their points by making that seem true which they knew to be false, and distorting the law and rendering it abortive; he did not believe that the average politicians regarded everything, no matter how disreputable, as "fair in politics;" he did not believe that the statesmanship of the world was a refined system of chicanery, and that statesmen were a lot of high-toned gamblers, who would not hesitate to steal the trump-card, if it were necessary to carry their points; in short, he did not believe that all men were naturally dissemblers.

And women, he regarded as possessing all the magnanimous traits of men, without the angular points of character which the sterner business of the world gives to men. If he regarded men as diamonds whose sharp corners had not been rounded off, he regarded women as polished jewels. He would as soon have suspected that the sun might rise some morning divested of its power to give forth light and heat, as to have supposed that the average woman could be anything else but virtuous. To his exaggerated standard of estimation, woman was all he had conceived man to be, besides possessing the softness, the spotless virtue, the angelic love, attributed to the sex by the most imaginative and eulogistic poets.

While he looked upon humanity as so high-toned, he labored to achieve the admiration and respect of mankind as the greatest of human attainments. And here, had he stopped to think, was a refutation of the high estimation he had formed of human nature, in himself. For was not this very anxiety to gain applause and esteem for himself, a selfishness on his part that he did not believe existed to a large extent among men? Had mankind been as good as the standard which he had formed, he would have had little thought of the admiration and respect that he himself might win. He would have thought only how he might contribute to the general welfare, and the idea of gaining applause and esteem for himself would never have entered his mind. It is true that the admiration and respect which he thought of gaining, was that which is obtained by good actions which benefit humanity; but still this very desire for good opinions should have been proof to him of the inherent selfishness of human nature, and should have taught him that he had formed a false notion thereof, and set his standard too high. He had an estimation so hyperborean that a discovery of its falsity was likely to place humanity entirely without the pale of his sympathy, and render him utterly regardless of making further effort to win the applause of mankind by improving his usefulness.

While he regarded human nature so highly, the applause and respect of men and women were things worth working for, from sunrise till the waning hours told the approach of another day. To feel that he had the esteem and admiration of his fellow-citizens was much more satisfactory to him than to fill coffers with gold. Nor was he insensible to the influence of the softer passions inspired by the sex he respected so highly. An estimable young woman, from the distant city, who was in the habit of spending her summers in the village where Horace Lackfathe resided, had enkindled in his heart a passion stronger than his desire for fame. And she, knowing the consideration in which he was held in his native village, was proud of his attentions. She was understood to be a teacher, who sought recreation during the summer vacation in the pure atmosphere of the hills and meadows adjacent to the village. Thus the conditions of the two were apparently not dissimilar, and they were evidently well suited to each other. Miss Charity Faithful was doubtless destined to become Mrs. Lackfathe.

Horace Lackfathe had not mingled enough with men. He had lived too much in the ideal world of books, and his own enthusiastic thoughts. This, combined with a peculiar temperament, rendered him a hyperborean being, different in a measure from those around. He could comprehend only the better part of human nature, and looked upon all deviations from his standard simply as monstrosities, which were the exceptions to the general rule; just as he would view an unusual visitation of frost in mid-summer. So long as his intercourse with the world only occasionally brought him in contact with an individual who did not come up to his standard, he considered it merely as one of those exceptional cases which are to be met with in everything.

A change came over him; and from the most elevated opinion of mankind, he fell into the very opposite extreme of regarding them with universal distrust. It might truly be said that he had no faith at all in the race. Nor was this want of faith in others attended by a sort of self-righteousness on his part. Looking around upon the numerous temptations in which men fell—defaulting cashiers, merchants swindling their creditors, politicians resorting to open and shameless corruption, statesmen stooping to tricks which he thought confined to the gambling dens, faithless husbands and wives,—he began to doubt whether there was a spark of real honor in human nature, and distrusted himself with the rest. He thought that, perhaps, he might also be led to give way to temptation, were he placed in certain situations. He began to be of the opinion that nothing but the most severe discipline could reform mankind, and that none but those who laid down for themselves a stern code of morality, and stuck to it rigidly, could escape the common demoralization.

The change had not come suddenly over Horace Lackfathe. The war of the Rebellion was the first rude shock to his finely organized sensibilities. He was confounded that men were bad enough to attempt the overthrow of the Republic which he adored. Then the demoralization which attends all wars still further lessened his faith in human nature. The corruption that will always follow in the handling of large sums of money, and the execution of herculean contracts, revealed the worst shade of human nature in its unspeakable deformity. The statesmanship of the world was also illustrated in its hypocrisy, selfishness, and time-serving expedients. The veil was rudely torn from what he supposed to be the angelic nature of women and the unswerving morality of men. Wives whose husbands had gone to fight the battles of their country were often found faithless to their marriage vows, and husbands who had gotten beyond the influence of their family circles frequently forgot that they owed allegiance to the one who presided over their distant homes.

The rude world to which Horace Lackfathe had just wakened up, was not the Utopian one of his day dreams. It was not the world that had inspired his aims to gain its good opinion and high consideration. He was gradually coming to regard its good opinion as scarcely worth laboring for, and consequently his exertions slackened. To him, now, the high opinion of men in general seemed nothing more than the applause of a demoralized crowd given over to moral perdition; the consideration of statesmen and men of high degree seemed but the approbation of the aristocracy of transgressors; the admiration of women seemed but the flattery of those in whose virtue he had been deceived. So he almost ceased his efforts to build himself up in the estimation of such a world, and thus his talents, which were of the first order, were allowed to remain in abeyance. He still, however, continued to perform the duties of his position in a correct and upright manner.

At the date we introduced him to the reader in his strange adventure in the Catskill mountains, it was some time after the close of the Rebellion, when he was something over thirty years of age; and as subsequent events will show, he had not by any means improved in his estimation of his fellow-men. And, indeed, if he took public men as the standard of human excellence, he had little reason to think the race had improved since the beginning of the war.

CHAPTER IV.

THE LEECH CLUB.

Some days after the adventure of Horace Lackfathe in the Catskills, a company was gathered in a richly furnished parlor in a neighboring city. The appearance and surroundings of this company rather betokened superfluous riches than refinement. The parlors, though furnished to profusion, presented a tawdry rather than a beautiful appearance. Costly furniture was incongruously thrown together without that nice display of taste usually shown by people who have learned to appreciate such elegancies, and arrange them with a view to harmony. The dress and physiognomy of the company seemed as much out of character as the rooms and furniture. There was a superfluity of diamonds, jewelry, rich clothes, silks, laces, etc.; apparently donned by the wearers in order to get on their persons as much as possible of the finery of the day, because they had the money to pay for it—and having but one life to live, desired to enjoy as much of their riches as possible. The carriage and presence of these people might have led a stranger to suspect that the attaches of the kitchen of the establishment had, in the absence of the real owners thereof, loaded themselves incongruously with the fine apparel of their masters, and were playing at gentleman and lady in the parlors for a short time. Nevertheless, there were present several high officials, including a member of Congress and a member of the State Legislature. We shall find there are some here whose acquaintance we briefly made in that mysterious mansion in the Catskills. Mr. Swellup, addressing the Congressman, said:

"Mr. Longterm, now that Congress has adjourned, and you have honored the Leech Club with a few days' residence at their rooms in the City, I hope you will also allow us the pleasure of your company for a longer stay at our Club House in the Catskills."

"Indeed, I was not aware that you had a Club House in the Catskills. Something rustic, I suppose? not on such a magnificent scale as your Club House in the City?"

"Well, not quite; but it is not a poverty-stricken mansion, I can tell you. It is built of the native stone of the mountains, but the inside finishing and furniture are as good as this very building we are now in. It is in a secluded valley, surrounded on all sides by a swift running stream of water, which, for a novelty, is crossed by a drawbridge, so as to remind us somewhat of the habitations of the old feudal barons. There is good fishing in the streams, and the mountain forests are not destitute of game. Bears, and even occasionally a panther, are found."

"And," said Mr. Flitaway, "there are other means of excitement besides the bears and panthers. And our stone building with its iron doors and shutters, and iron roof, and drawbridge, affords us other satisfaction than that of imagining ourselves in a feudal castle. Some of the strangest noises and sights are sometimes heard and seen in those mountains. Some believe that the mountains are a favorite haunt of spirits, while others believe that they are infested by a gang of robbers or counterfeiters, who get up supernatural appearances in order to frighten people from frequenting the mountains, and so disturbing them in the pursuit of their vocation. Figures resembling men have been seen to disappear in the face of a solid ledge of rock, where, upon examination, no aperture except a mere seam could be found. Some, who are not superstitious, but have witnessed with their own eyes this unaccountable disappearance of what looked like men, into the solid rock, try to explain it on the supposition that there is a gang of men who have caves in the rocks, and have some powerful machinery within by which they can raise a large rock which forms the door of the cave, into which they quickly retire, when the great door is suddenly closed. For my part, I think it requires greater faith to believe this theory than to believe that the mysterious figures are supernatural beings."

"Indeed," said Mr. Longterm, "you have excited my curiosity so that I shall certainly accept your invitation to visit this wonderful region. With angling for trout, hunting bears, and hob-nobbing with ghosts, I doubt not that I shall be able to kill time for a week or two. But if I should get worsted in an argument with the ghostly crew, and be compelled to retreat into the castle, I fear that your drawbridge, and iron doors and shutters, will be but a poor protection against those spirits, who go right into the solid rock."

"As to that, whatever these apparitions are, ghosts or men, they have never yet made their appearance inside of our Club House, nor even across the drawbridge."

"Perhaps you keep the draw open, and these ghosts, like cats, may not like to wet their feet by wading the stream," suggested Mr. Longterm.

"Indeed," said Miss Gossamer, "you won't be so much disposed to jest about this matter if you encounter these demons in the mountains on some moonlight evening. Only a short time before we left, a stranger got benighted in the mountains in one of those terrible thunder storms, and by some means straggled upon the Club House; and when he entered he looked as though he had just had a tilt with the Evil One. We have since found out that he saw strange things in the mountains."

"And," said Mr. Swellup, "this stranger, who gave his name as Horace Lackfathe, is about as much of a puzzle to me as the ghosts. He claims to be a lawyer by profession, and says he came out into the mountains for the improvement of his health. He is a man of good education; and we have prevailed on him to remain with us during the summer and teach the children of some members of the Club, who don't care to have them lose too much time from their studies."

"Just the thing," said Mr. Longterm. "My two boys are preparing for college, and want to improve their time."

"And," said Mrs. Grandola, "he can introduce you to the demons, as I don't doubt but he is a relation of theirs."

Mr. Longterm smiled, and then remarked to Mr. Swellup: "By the way, I judge by the number of splendid establishments kept up by the Leech Club, that it is more profitable to be a municipal officer or a member of the Legislature than a member of Congress; as the members of your Club are mostly city officials, or connected with the State Government."

"In that you are right," said Mr. Swellup. "I had much rather be an Alderman or a member of the Legislature than to be a United States Senator."

"But the pay is not so large."

"Oh! no; but there are perquisites that more than make up the difference; as you can judge from the fact that the members of the Leech Club have nearly all amassed large fortunes from their official positions."

"And what are these perquisites, pray?"

"One large item is for legal services."

"But you are not all lawyers?"

"Oh! no, a man can act as attorney for another without being a lawyer. For instance," continued Mr. Swellup, "in the city there are large contracts to be put out on the various public works. It is a very simple matter for a man to act as attorney for any one who wants to get a contract. The profits are generally good on such work, and the contractor can afford to pay an Alderman liberally for acting as his attorney in obtaining for him the job. Why, I have known a contractor to realize a profit of $50,000 on a small job of cleaning two or three streets for six months. Of this sum about $40,000 goes to the Alderman or other official who acts as attorney, and the contractor gets the balance. I have known an official to make $10,000 for legal services for a contractor just for the plastering of one room in a public building. The contractor's whole profits on such a job would probably be about $15,000, he making $5,000, and the city official getting $10,000 for legal services. On the larger contracts, such as the opening of streets, the improvement of parks, and the erection of large public buildings, I have known the profits to run up into the hundreds of thousands, and even millions, on a single job. Invariably the official who acts as attorney for the contractor gets much the larger portion of the profits, as he should, for without his influence the contractor never could have obtained the job. So it is on all public works. The contractors must have attorneys to look after their interests; and who can better act as such attorney than those who have positions in the City Government?

"As to members of the Legislature, they also have excellent opportunities to make good fees by acting as attorneys. Railroad companies and other powerful corporations have bills which they desire passed. It is very necessary to have attorneys to look after such things. Certainly, no man is better qualified for acting as attorney in getting a bill passed than a member of the Legislature. Railroad and other large corporations are in fact the real Government of the country. If a man wants to be elected to the Legislature, he has need of the aid of any railroad corporation that may be in his district. The railroad corporations actually choose legislative and executive officers; and these officials may in reality consider themselves elected as the attorneys of these companies. Therefore, the most of men when they go to the Legislature are engaged beforehand as the attorneys of railroads and other rich corporations, and it is their bounden duty to act as such. But while the legislators are the legal servants of these corporations, even though the latter did not pay them another dollar after aiding in their election, the companies always pay the members of the Legislature liberally for legal services every time they want a bill passed. There is nothing mean about these rich corporations. I tell you, sir, the railroads are the ruling power in the country, and we might as well admit it first as last. There is not half the ability manifested in our State Government as in some railroad corporations that I could name. I sometimes think it is hardly necessary for the Legislature to meet at all, for it generally but registers the decrees of the railroad corporations.

"Why not let the Presidents of the railroads get together, and say what they want, and let the legislators stay at home? The country would save money by it; for it has to pay the expense of getting the Legislature together to do what the railroads require, and the latter have to pay legal fees to the members; and then the companies are obliged to charge the public higher for fares and freights in order to make up for the expense of legislation. I tell you, sir, if you would just let the railroads and other rich corporations take the Government in hand, they would run it with less expense than it is administered at present. Nor would the members of the Legislature be turned loose upon the world, without employment or support. They could be engaged at a liberal compensation to help take charge of the railroads."

Thus spoke this model statesman, Mr. Swellup. To such a venal pass had the politicians of his school come, that they talked among themselves of the most outrageous acts of public robbery and corruption, as unblushingly as if they were the most legitimate business affairs of life. Surrounded there in his own parlors by every luxury which his uncultivated taste and ill-gotten wealth could procure, with the exception of a certain low shrewdness, he possessed no intellectual advantages over the obscure rabble from which he emerged only a few years ago. Destitute of all sense of public propriety, this man was at the head of a political faction which controlled a large State. The shameless acts of this clique were, with the exception of a few of the most criminal robberies of the public treasury, done as openly as if they were entirely legitimate. No effort was made to conceal proceedings which should have sent certain officials to the State Prison.

It appeared as though the infamous clique represented by Mr. Swellup were either so ignorant that they did not appreciate the scandal of their own transactions, or else they hoped to make roguery respectable by practicing it openly, and making it common. Thus the depravity of the young men of their set, growing up around them, was astounding. The clique lived in an unbounded, gorgeous extravagance, supported chiefly by public plunder; and they plied their vocation as openly as the respectable portion of the community did their honest callings. Their aped-gentility was rendered the more detestable by a coarse vulgarity. Strong in the possession of political power, they carried themselves with an insolence as galling to the honest tax-payers from whom they had stolen their wealth, as the rattling of the chains is to the slave bound to the one who robs him of the fruits of his honest labor. These unfledged noblemen of the pilfered treasury spoke of those who made any pretensions to honesty, with contempt, and exalted any man who, by shrewd rascality, managed to amass a fortune. Honesty was with them a by-word, and they spoke of "stealings" as the great desideratum of any position, public or private, with as great nonchalance as if such were a part of the recognized perquisites of any shrewd man who should have the handling of funds.

And it was rather discouraging for those who rely greatly on human nature, to observe how fast this faction were infusing their turpitude into the community. People actually began to view with indifference the shameless lives of this clique. Had they endeavored to rob the public treasury secretly, they would soon have been detected and brought to grief. But the long, open and successful pursuit of their nefarious calling, caused people gradually to regard them as being engaged in legitimate practices. Their great wealth enabled them to daze the less thoughtful, and corrupt the weak and venal. It may seem strange, but it is true, that what before had been looked upon as criminal, was getting to be regarded as right, and a matter of course; simply because this clique had openly practiced infamy, and thrown around it the glamour of wealth. It is therefore evident that no monstrosity is too absurd or infamous to pass for a time unchallenged, provided it is attended with success.

The more thoughtful portion of the community looked upon the doings of this clique in powerless horror. The clique had made politics and office-holding so disreputable that men of reputation shrunk from taking any part in them. There was such shrewdness mingled with their rascality that they seemed to be constantly gaining strength. They scattered their stolen wealth freely in every direction, resorting to specific bribery where that was best, and to insidious bribery where that was more expedient. They extended a lavish patronage to the newspaper press, and thus insidiously propitiated that powerful engine to their interests. Men controlling powerful journals, who would have scorned a specific bribe, were thus subtly won over by receiving liberal contracts in the way of public printing. The clique were constantly increasing their ranks by taking into close communion those who were men after their own hearts. They were extending their ramifications into other States, and obtaining a foothold in the halls of the Federal Government. They had united their fortunes and forces with the unscrupulous heads of powerful railroad companies and other great corporations; so that the assertion of Mr. Swellup that these were the real Government of the country, had a shade of truth. Every rich corporation, which happened to be controlled by unscrupulous men, who needed any legislation to aid their nefarious designs, or feared any adverse enactments, were either a part of this clique, or else were its tributaries.

In a word, their dazzling wealth and unconcealed venality had blinded the multitude; their money was ready to hire the venal to corrupt the ballot-box; the apparent hopelessness of the situation, and the unutterable ill-repute into which politics had fallen, had driven honest men to the shades of private life, glad if they could preserve a moiety of their effects from the rapacious crew; they moulded the venal of all parties to subserve their base purposes, and thus had their friends in every political organization; and so a legalized highway robbery held high carnival, and men began to ask, "Is this what is called a Republican Government?"

CHAPTER V.

THE CASTLE OF THE LEECH CLUB.

As might be expected, when Horace Lackfathe retired to bed in the mysterious dwelling in the Catskills, his mind was racked by a good many conflicting thoughts. At first he was disposed to surmise that he had fallen upon a den of junketing outlaws, and was in doubt with regard to his safety. But a little reflection satisfied him that this could not be so; for he reasoned that, notwithstanding he had wandered a long distance inland, he could not be at most more than a few miles from the haunts of civilization, and that a building of this size could not long remain unknown to the wanderers among the Catskills. He was not superstitious enough to believe that such a structure could be the creation of supernatural agencies, which could obliterate it at as short notice as they called it into existence. He therefore rightly reasoned that the building must be known to the people who inhabited the country near by. As to his safety, he concluded that, were the inmates disposed to deal violently with him, he would incur just as much danger in attempting to leave as in remaining, for he could not depart without their knowledge. Moreover, in his exhausted condition, he felt that he would rather risk the consequences in the building, than again to brave the dangers and terrors of a nightly journey through the mountains. He soon fell asleep from very exhaustion.

The sun was high in the heavens when he awoke. Making as respectable a toilet as he could, considering his drenching of the previous night, he descended to the ground floor of the building. He soon came in contact with the people of the establishment, and was civilly treated, and conducted to a room of good size, where breakfast was served. There seemed to be no particular regularity or concert among the inmates in partaking of this meal. They came and went as suited their inclinations. Ladies and gentlemen lounged at the tables, sipping their coffee, and partaking of the viands languidly, indulging in a little chat, or remaining silent, as comported with their mood. Having satisfied himself with substantial comforts, Horace left the dining-room; and as he did so, he met a civil-appearing man, who politely informed him that he was welcome to remain in the establishment until he should feel rested from the evident exhaustion that he must have suffered during his previous night's wanderings in the mountains. Horace explained briefly that he had been making a short stay at one of the many boarding-houses in the Catskills, had strolled off to one of the high peaks, and become lost, and benighted in the mountains. When he spoke of the strange and apparently supernatural sights he had seen, and sounds he had heard, the gentleman's countenance wore an undefinable expression, but he did not manifest surprise or incredulity. Horace ventured a few questions in regard to the existence of so luxurious a dwelling in so obscure a situation in the mountains, premising that it seemed almost like the creation of genii or fairies; but he obtained no real satisfaction as to who erected the building, or for what purpose it was built, any further than that it was resorted to by some wealthy men from a distant city. After gaining what information he could, and briefly viewing such of the rooms as he passed through, Horace walked out into the open air.

It was one of those bright summer mornings so common in mountain regions after the air has undergone the purifying influence of rain and thunder. The sky presented a pure, unadulterated blue; the foliage on the mountain sides, cleansed and refreshed by the recent rain, was of a rich green; and the mountain streams sparkled as if with diamonds washed down from the rocks. The birds sang with the sprightliness that only the feathered tribe can exhibit after a heavy rain has been followed by a brilliant clearing-up. The bees went humming about from flower to flower, adding their cheerful song of industry to the warbling of the birds.

The building stood in a most enchanting spot. To the east the mountains parted into a deep gorge, through which the morning sun streamed with all the glory and brilliancy of its summer rays. On the other hand were two other breaks in the mountains, the one gorge opening in a direction a little north of west, the other a little south of west. Thus was the building situated in a position for the inmates to witness the most enchanting effects of sunrise and sunset in the mountains.

Down each of the two gorges mentioned as opening to the west, flowed a rapid stream of water, of considerable size. A short distance to the west of the building these two streams united, and after running a short distance as one, the stream parted into two currents, flowing one to the right, and the other to the left of the small plateau on which the house stood, and a short distance below leaping in two splendid cascades down into a charming little lake of sixty or seventy acres, its waters cut into irregular shapes by the jutting mountain headlands. Thus the house stood in the centre of an island of about six acres with a swiftly-running stream on either side, and two beautiful cascades and a lake in front. The little island on which the house stood had been partly cleared of the native forest trees, only enough having been left standing to afford ample shade. The grounds were partly kept and partly in their native wildness. As the ground descended in front of the house, it had there for a short distance been artificially formed into terraces, after which it was left in its natural state, descending rapidly to the shore of the lake. In parts of the grounds, there were walks and parterres, the latter blooming with cultivated flowers. In the uncultivated portions the wild flowers grew in their native luxuriance; and thus the wild honey-suckle, the dogwood and the countless and almost nameless flora of the woods, were brought into close contrast with the fuchsia, the aster, and the dahlia. In a spacious greenhouse were many rare plants.

Ducks, geese and swans were swimming in the lake, and fowls of various kinds were seen wandering about the grounds, or hovering around the hennery. The notes of these, if not musical, at least helped to vary the monotony of the lonely situation. On the lake were symmetrical boats, with awnings to protect from the sun those who sought pleasure in sailing.

Proceeding from the inspection of details to the more prominent features of the landscape, the beholder could not fail to remark that the scene was one of almost incomparable grandeur. The building stood in a sort of triangular valley, hemmed in by lofty peaks, separated by the opening gorges we have mentioned. The sides of these mountains were diversified with tremendous rocky precipices, gorges, and tracts of timber. The latter consisted partly of evergreens, and partly of hardwood timber. The rich, softer green of the deciduous trees was commingled with the sombre foliage of the evergreens; and the many variations of shade imparted by the sun to the billowy sea of verdure, rendered the effect indescribable. Owing to the various and irregular positions of the mountains, as the sun poured his brilliant rays upon the landscape, some portions of it stood in deep shade, some in a shade of less degree, while some reflected the full power of the sun's fervent beams. The deep gorges reposed as under sombre clouds, and the mountain crests looked like ridges cropping out with gold. It was a scene for a painter.

Horace turned from the magnificent scene to an inspection of the dwelling. Though a good-sized stone building, constructed somewhat in the Gothic style, there was nothing especially formidable about its appearance. The outer walls were of stone, in the dressing of which there had been no great deal of pains taken. The doors and window-blinds, though painted to look like wood, on a near inspection were found to be iron. The blinds were made in the open, lattice fashion, like those of any ordinary dwelling. They were made with strong fastenings; and the inmates of the house at night might have plenty of air, and still feel secure that no one could readily enter the building from the outside. This might have been a necessary precaution in so lonely a place. The roof, though painted to look like slate, was composed of sheet iron plates. The building was two stories high, with sleeping apartments in the attic, and would accommodate more people than one might suppose at first sight.

CHAPTER VI.

HORACE MAKES SOME NEW ACQUAINTANCES.

As Horace leisurely inspected the premises, he was suddenly startled by a voice just over his shoulder, saying:

"My good friend, you must not be astonished at anything you see here."

Horace turned as if he expected to see one of the ghostly crew who had haunted his wanderings on the previous evening, and after apparently assuring himself that he was addressed by a creature of flesh and blood, replied:

"No, indeed, since last night, I should not be at all surprised to see a regiment of men march forth from yonder solid precipice."

"From what you say," responded the stranger, "I

guess you have been favored with some of the strange sights that have been so often seen in these mountains."

"I have been living in a crowded city for a year past," said Horace, "and came out here into the mountains for the improvement of my physical health; but I fear, when I return, I shall have need of a physician who can 'minister to a mind diseased'; for after last night's adventures, and what I have seen here, I am almost led to doubt my own soundness of mind, or to think I have been, and am still, dreaming."

"Well," said the other, "if seeing strange things in the mountains constitutes craziness, you have plenty of company in your insanity. As for what you see here, it is a solid reality, as you will willingly testify by the time you have tasted the hospitalities of the establishment for a week."

"But, how is it that such an elegantly-furnished house is found in this out-of-the-way place, which, however delightful the landscape viewed from here, is reached—at least by me—in a manner as terrific as crossing the mythological river Styx?"

"Oh! it is only a resort fixed up by some gentlemen, where they can come and rusticate and have a first-rate time during the summer months. As to the strange sights you speak of, they are not often seen, and they rather add to the novelty of the situation. Occasionally, a person or a party of two or three, will come in and report having seen the most astounding things; and then the whole house, especially those who have never seen anything of the kind, will gather around and hear the wonderful tale, and all sorts of conjectures will be made as to the origin of the marvelous appearances. Some conjecture that there is a gang of counterfeiters here in the mountains, which I don't believe. Others regard them as spiritual manifestations, such as we have heard much of in the papers of late years. You know, spiritualists believe that certain localities are at times the especial resort of spirits, which, for reasons best known to themselves, cut up all sorts of unaccountable antics. For my part, I believe that many of these reports of strange things seen, result from the excited imaginations of those who are always ready to convert a shapeless rock or bush into a bugaboo; or often, perhaps, the inventions of those who like to recite a marvelous tale for the delectation of a gaping circle of listeners. Still, it must be admitted that some things have been seen here which cannot be accounted for from a human standpoint. Such, though, I believe to have been very rare occurrences."

"I," said Horace, "have been rather disposed to scout at the stories of mysterious manifestations such as have been reported from various parts of the country during the last few years. But I confess just now to being a little staggered. It certainly is admitted by all reasonable men that there are some apparently supernatural manifestations that have never been explained, but that is not saying that they never will be."

"There is," rejoined the other, "a legend extant in this section of country, that might furnish the text for many marvelous tales. It is respecting a man who lived some miles from where we are, before the Revolutionary war. He was a large landed proprietor, and in those days, as you are aware, it was a common thing to have bound white servants, who were as completely subject to their masters as were the slaves of the South before the emancipation. This man had a female servant, who, while compelled to give the employment of her hands to her arbitrary master, gave her heart to another individual. As a natural result, the girl ran away with her lover. The master pursued on horse-back, captured the girl, and tied her to his horse's tail. He then mounted his horse, and rode for home, the girl being compelled to march on behind like a captive hitched to the chariot of a Roman conqueror. A terrible fate awaited the poor girl; and a more terrible retribution was to be visited on the perpetrator of the cruel deed. The horse became frightened, ran away, and the life was dashed out of the poor captive upon the merciless rocks. The vindictive master was tried for murder, and found guilty. But owing to the wealth and influence of his family, the court was prevailed upon to postpone the execution of the sentence of death until he should reach the age of ninety-nine years. He was allowed to reside on his estate, but was condemned always to wear a cord around his neck, as a reminder of the fate that ultimately awaited him. He was also bound to appear before the court once a year, to hear a reiteration of the sentence. It would naturally have been supposed that one with such a sentence hanging over him would have fallen into premature decay, and that the canker-worm of remorse would have eaten away the vitals of life, long before the time appointed for the ever-present cord about his neck to be tightened upon the scaffold. But he apparently lived to suffer, an outcast from society, a prey to a consuming conscience, and the recipient of spectral visitations. The night winds as they rustled about his dwelling, were laden with sad sighs; a white cow, which had been a pet of the murdered girl, would frequently be seen wandering among the rocks, and lowing mournfully, but she always vanished into air on being approached; a large dog which had often received kindnesses at the girl's hands, would frequently stand looking toward the house and howling, but those who tried to coax the animal into friendliness, found they were talking to a spectre; sometimes a maiden would be seen standing on a distant rock, with a lighted candle, singing mournfully, or uttering cries of distress; frequently a horse would be seen dashing past, dragging behind him a female, mangled and bleeding, and uttering agonizing cries for help.

"Death refused to come to the aid of the man living under the terrible condemnation; whose days were a monotonous routine of withering sorrow and remorse, and whose nights were haunted by a constant, shadowy reenactment of scenes resembling the crime he had committed, or visitations from the spirit of the murdered girl, or the spectral appearances of the sympathizing dumb brutes which had loved her while living. The condemned man lived on from youth to middle age, gliding into the decline of life, and still the venom of remorse could not eat away his vitals, nor could his physical system be exhausted by a constant subjection to the terrors of two worlds—for it must be borne in mind that he lived on the confines of the material and the spiritual universe, subject to the shadowy terrors of the one, which ever kept before him the semblance of his wicked deed, and the real tangible terrors of the other, which ever kept about his neck the cord that was ultimately to strangle him. Like Cain, his punishment was greater than he could bear, but there was no alternative but to bear it. The generation which had been conversant with the circumstances of the crime, passed away, and still the old man lived quiet and inoffensive, but never knowing what it was to enjoy the sympathy of his fellow-citizens. His life was an anomaly. He apparently belonged to neither this world nor the next. He could neither penetrate beyond the gloom which hedges the dark Plutonian river, nor bask in the sunshine of this sublunary abode. He was over ninety years old, and still the people thought he would reach his ninety-ninth year, when his sentence would be executed. But not only had the generation who knew intimately of his crime, as well as the Court which sentenced him, passed away; the Government of the country was also changed. The Republic had taken the place of the Colonies, and had any one been disposed to enforce the punishment, there was no Court competent to take cognizance of a sentence passed seventy-five years before. The old man finally died peacefully in his bed, at the age of more than one hundred years; and if the object of the sentence was simply punishment, the spirit of the law was certainly carried out a hundred-fold."

"But," said Horace, after listening attentively to this singular tale, "you do not mean to say that the spirits of the murdered girl, and her sympathizing cows, dogs and horses, as well as the shade of the old man, still cling tenaciously to these mountains? As for the girl, I should think that, after the old man's death, she would no longer have occasion to 'revisit the glimpses of the moon, and make night hideous' in this locality; and as for the old man, I should think he had seen trouble enough in these parts, without desiring to come back here."

"No, no, my friend," said the other, "I have no such idea. I have only related to you a legend of the Catskills as it has been told to me. Indeed, if wicked and cruel deeds cause spirits to break over the confines of the unknown world, there is abundant reason why they should appear just now. I know men who go unsentenced, unhung and unpunished—for not even their consciences seem to trouble them—whose crimes are ten-fold blacker than that of the old man mentioned in the story.

And if dark deeds cause the shades of men to walk the earth after they are dead, I know some men now living who will make first-class ghosts one of these days."

"'It needs no ghost to tell us that,'" said Horace.

"And," said the other, "here comes a coterie, who, if their sins are a qualification, will make a lively band of ghosts for this region at some future time, should the race of Catskill shadows depreciate or run out, and need renewing."

Horace and his new acquaintance were here joined by eight or ten men, richly attired, who were evidently out for a morning walk. The foremost one addressed Horace's companion, in the mincing tones of uncertain pronunciation, affected by the city swell. A noted feature of this dialect is to leave off the " r " at the termination of a syllable or word. Another is to put a strong accent on syllables that are not properly accented. In this way the swell language has a peculiar, mincing expression, which the users of it think is very impressive and refined. Horace's companion was known as Mr. Graphic, and this name was pronounced by the swell as if it were spelled, Grawf-feek, with both syllables accented.

"Aw, Mistah Grawf-feek, a fine day foh sketching. I wondah you are not engaged with youah brush and pencil this mo'ning."

"Oh! Mr. Sindandy," replied Mr. Graphic, "I have found very agreeable employment in showing this stranger the lions, or rather the pet wolf and bear, hereabouts, and explaining, as far as possible, the whys and wherefores of things which naturally must seem strange to him."

"You say truly, Mistah Grawf-feek. It must seem odd to a strangah to find a palace hea in the mountains. But we could show him mattahs and things pahtaining to the Leech Club, much strangah than this. My friend," (addressing Horace) "did you evah hea of the Leech Club befoah ?"

Horace replied that he had heard some vague reports respecting the Club, but knew little about it.

"Well, moi friend, a man who is admitted into membahship of the Leech Club, may considah his foahtune made. You might say, moi friend, that the Leech Club is the actual Govahment of the State, and it will one of these days govern the nation. It also numbahs among its membahs some of the fi'st railroad men in the country. We have Club houses in seve'al States, both in country and in the large cities; but this one in the Catskills is one of ouah favorite summah resoahts."

"You must," said Horace, "have a mine of wealth to draw on, in order to support so many establishments, provided they are all as splendid as this one is in the interior."

"This, moi friend, is nothing. It is no moah than one of the neighbo'ing, rustic fa'm houses compa'ed to some of our city establishments. The palaces of Europe are not moah splendid. As for suppoahting them, you may well say we have a mine of wealth to draw on. I, you see, am a young man, but I have served the country and the public in seve'al diffe'ent capacities. I have been to the Legislacha, whea I made a good thing. I have had city contracts; I have acted as refe'ee in cases at law, whea the fees are la'ge; I have been connected with railroad co'porations; and you must know that such officials receive liberal compensation; for the public must pay its faithful servants. You must have observed this fact, that no class of men do so well as those who draw thea pay from the public. And the reason is clea; for whea you are wo'king for one employah, he may find time to higgle about the price; but the public consists of so many, no one is going to scrutinize things so closely. Besides, even if they pay a little too much, it is divided up among so many that no one feels it. Therefoah, we might as well have a good price when we wo'k for the public. Nothing like serving youah country, moi friend, for youah country's good, and moah especially for youah own."

"You speak," said Horace, "of having made a good thing in the Legislature. But the pay of members of that body is very small—scarcely enough to pay their expenses. I don't see how they can lay up anything out of their salaries."

Mr. Sindandy drew a long "whew!" as if in commiseration of Horace's ignorance, and said:

"I see, moi friend, you are not much acquainted with public affai's. The stated pay of a membah of the Legislacha will not pay for his segahs. If that was all he could make there, he might bettah go to the pooah-house. You fo'get that some co'poration or individual is interested in almost every bill that passes, and that it requiahs wo'k to get bills through. And do you suppose those who give thea time and influence to accomplish all this legislation, are going to do it for nothing? It is true that there are many in the Legislacha who have no influence thea, and as they can do little towa'ds aiding legislation, they obtain but little for thea services except their regulah salary. Such men don't amount to much in the Legislacha, and they soon get tired of serving there.

"It is not a man's talents so much that give him influence in the Legislacha, as it is his connections. It depends on the chain of influences he can bring to beah on legislation, how much he is to be thought of in that body. It is something, moi friend, to be a membah of the Leech Club, to have influence in the Legislacha. This Club has a hundred influences it can bring to beah on legislation. There is hardly a section of the State in which the Club does not control some interests. The membahs of the Club control railroads, and factories, and canals, and best of all, the patronage of the State. Now, suppose the Club want a bill passed. We can say to membahs from the different sections of the State: You must vote for this bill, or such and such a railroad will not be careful to serve the interests of youah constituents. The chief passenger trains will give youah place the go-by, and the local tariff of freights will be raised. We can say to othah membahs: You must vote for this bill, or such and such a factory will stop, and a la'ge numbah of youah constituents will be thrown out of employment in the dead of wintah. The Club controls so many railroads, factories, mines and othah la'ge interests, that we can bring these influences to beah. We can control men interested in banks, by promising them the State funds to deposit; and the State patronage gives us a levah with which we expect some day to move even the National Govahment. But it would take me a week to recount all the engines we have for influencing State legislation.

"So you see, moi friend, that any one who wants a

bill passed is bound to come for aid to some membah of the Legislacha who belongs to the Leech Club. No mattah what the bill may be, we can pass it or kill it. You may reasonably suppose that we don't give our valuable services for nothing. It is a great deal of trouble for us to go around and drum up the votes for the passage of a bill, and it is no moah than right that we should be paid for extra wo'k. While we are doing this wo'k, the othah membahs are enjoying thea ease, and it is perfectly fair that we should have extra pay, and there is nothing illegal about it.

"You see, moi friend, that talent for speech-making is but a feathah in the scale, when weighed against the substantial influences of the Leech Club. I would rathah be able to wield the influence of this Club in ordah to carry any measha through the Legislacha, than to possess the eloquence of Webstah, Clay, Patrick Henry, and William Pitt, combined. Sometimes a man will get up in the Legislacha, and make a fine speech on some bill; and if we membahs who belong to the Leech Club are opposed to him, we laugh in our sleeves to hear him waste his breath. Aftah he gets through, we control the vote on the bill as we want it, and the speech has no moah effect than if he had spoken it heah in the mountains to the rocks and trees.

"But I have talked sufficient to give you an idea how a man may make a good thing in the Legislacha, and still take nothing for which he does not rendah an equivalent in real honest wo'k. I will now introduce you to moi friends hea, who belong to the Leech Club. As you get acquainted with them, you will see that we do not confine ouah membahship to the higah classes. We find useful membahs in all classes of society. The main condition is that a membah shall be a representative man of his class, and be able to influence them at an election."

Horace viewed the crowd with a quick, critical eye, and mentally came to the conclusion that these must have been admitted into the Leech Club for anything but their intellectual or moral qualifications. There were evidently among the number those who had been raised to their present elevation from the very slums of a large city, as well as those who had been fairly brought up, but were lacking in the elements of principle and self-respect, which invest the possessor with an appearance of manly dignity. Their rich dress comported oddly with their want of moral tone, and they appeared more like a band of freebooters than men who could walk boldly through the community, unchallenged by the administrators of the law. There were Irishmen, and Germans, and nonchalant Americans among the motley crew. As Horace shook their jeweled hands, he felt as if condemned by the demon of the mountains to fondle the venomous serpents called forth from the rocky dens, hooped with diamond rings culled from their impenetrable caves. No degree of ornamentation could have rendered their touch aught but loathsome.

"Glad to see yez, Mr. Lackfathe," said Patrick O'Gull, "and hope yez may be lucky enough to git to be a member of the Lache Club, that Mr. Sindandy has been tellin' yez aboot. Faith, an' the Club has made me forchin, it has. When I comed to this blessed land of liberty, I was as poor as Father O'Flaherty's cow what depended for her livin' on the gift of paratee skins from his congregashin; and the poor baste didn't git mooch, for the paple was so poor that they ginerally ate their paratees skins and all. Yez may be sure that when I comed to this country I had to work hard till I got to be a voter, and could bring to me back in me own ward a coople hundred as good b'ys wid the ballot as ever swinged pick, or handled a shillaly in a 'lection fight. Afther a while I got in wid the Lache Club, and they got me a contract to clane the streets in the city, and I made me ten thousand dollars in three months. Sin' that I've not had to swing the pick or shovel eny more at all, for the Club has always seen to it that I've had plenty of contracts and good pay. God bless America for the free ballot, and God bless the Lache Club, what knows how to apprasheate a man that sarves them and the pooblic well."

Here Otto Swillager took up the thread of conversation, addressing Horace:

"I zay, mine frent—vat you calls him?—ah! Mr. Laghvathe—mebbe you dinks Mr. O'Kull here kets all de tings vat ams goot, as de Leege Clubs gives to de beples. Put you petter not tink zo, I dells you. Vy, mine frent, ven I gooms from Germany, I no zo much as habs de bennies to py von glass lager. I vorks, and vorks, and vorks, and mine bocket geeps as embdy as never vas. Put pine-py I fints it pest to vills mine bocket mit votes, and den you pets I kets zelong. De Leege Club zay you zusht de man ve vants. I kets de contract, I geeps de zaloon, and I no hab to bay de licenz. I zoon fints dat de man vat garries de votes in de bocket, garries de moneys dare too. Eh!"

"Put a stopper on that rigmarole, you lager-tongued Dutchman!" said Jim Hardnuckle, a native American ornament of the worthy Club. "I thank my stars, pals, that I've not had to wade into the good graces of the Club through swill-barrels, lager-vats, gutters, and filthy snow-banks in the streets. These are the boys that have won my way to fortune,"—and he exhibited a couple of heavy-looking fists, shaking them so near the head of the Irishman, that the latter ejaculated:

"Arrah, ye blatherin spalpeen, what do yez mane?"

"No harm, Pat," said Jim. "Don't you remember the 'lection day when we cleaned out them challengers that was tryin' to bluff off from votin' the fifty emigrants just arrived from Ireland that you brought to the polls?"

"Yes, well do I, and yez behaved like a broth of a boy, as yez are, Jim."

"I reckon, Pat, you'd a' come out at the little end of the horn with your votes on that day, if it hadn't been for me and some of the other 'boys.'"

"Faith, and that we would. Ye're as yooseful as ony of us, Jim."

The party had proceeded to the shore of the lake heretofore mentioned, and some of them, among whom was Mr. Swillager, were seated in the shade on the rocks which jutted into the water. Whether Jim Hardnuckle was afraid he might become rusted in pugilistic science, or whether from mere force of habit, cannot at this time be definitely known, but he indulged in another flourish of his fists, this time bringing them into unpleasant proximity to the head of the German. The latter was evidently not so much accustomed to such things as the Irishman, for he dodged and swayed so far over that he lost his balance, and turned a summersault into the lake.

A clamor of alarm was raised by the company, the geese in the lake set up a cackling, the turkeys about the premises gobbled, the dogs barked, and all was commotion where only a moment before reigned the native stillness of the mountains. However well the German might have been trained in the art of drinking lager, and carrying votes in his pocket, his education respecting water had been sadly neglected; at least in regard to keeping his head above it. It was quite plain that he had never had much to do with water, judging from his general appearance and his fat, unwieldy person. It was evident that lager was his native element, and had he fallen into a lake of that liquor, it is probable that he would soon have extricated himself by drinking it dry. But, though he may have been of sufficient capacity to exhaust the lake in his huge person, water evidently did not agree with him, and so much of it would not remain on his stomach.

Floundering about in ten feet of water, clutching above the surface as if he expected to get hold of a sunbeam and thus sustain his huge body, he seemed in imminent danger of drowning, for none of his comrades appeared disposed to soil their gaudy plumage by plunging in to his rescue. Doubtless they feared to grapple in the water with such a huge hippopotamus. Mr. Sindandy looked on in mute, helpless despair, as if already taking an inventory of the number of votes that would be lost with the German, and placing the same to the account of profit and loss. The shore, but a few feet off, was like the bottle behind the counter to the poor, penniless inebriate, suffering from the effects of a debauch. He could almost touch it, but grasp it he could not. His case was a symbol of the fate that awaited the iniquitous organization to which he belonged. While seated on a footing apparently as secure as the eternal hills, he had all at once found himself standing on what was to him the same as nothing. His inactive comrades doubtless said to themselves: It cannot be possible that he can go under with the firm rocks just at his fingers' ends! And yet he was going under before their eyes, almost within their reach. The rocks are near, but he is not on the rocks. And so it will be with you, ye false

Leech Club! you may see the firm rocks of virtue all around you, but you are not standing on them. One of these days you will find your unstable foundations all at once slipping from under you, and yourselves floundering about in an element that you know not the nature of. You will find yourselves overwhelmed by a moral flood, to which you have so long been unaccustomed that you cannot swim in it. It will matter little then to look about you and say: We can almost touch with the tips of our fingers the engines of Government which we have so long run. It cannot be possible that we have lost our hold on these forever. See how close they are. Strain every nerve to get hold of them again. It cannot be possible that we must sink here with our feet almost on the rocks, and our hands almost grasping them. But you don't quite touch them, do you! and they might as well be a thousand miles off for all the good they do you. You might as well be struggling in mid-ocean as here with the firm ground you have walked on just beyond grasping reach, and the bottom of the lake which is engulfing you, just far enough down that your toes cannot touch it, and the friends you know, just far enough off not to be able to lend you a helping hand.

The struggling German was about sinking for the last time, and Horace and Mr. Graphic were about to rush in to the rescue, and thus do for him what his more intimate friends were too cowardly to do, when a large Newfoundland dog, which had been attracted to the spot by the splashing, plunged in, seized him by the clothing, and gave him such an impetus toward the shore, that the men standing there were able to get hold of him. He was dragged out in an unconscious, flabby condition, the starch having evidently been all water-soaked out of him. His companions immediately resorted to the most common methods of resuscitation in such cases.

"Here," said one, " is a barrel. Let's roll him on this. I guess it's an old lager-cask, and he'll be sure to smell the beer, and come to life."

In due course of time the German was restored to consciousness, and, feeling somewhat gorged with the quantity of water he had involuntarily swallowed, seemed to be in doubt whether he had just recovered from an inebriation caused by imbibing an extra quantity of his favorite beverage, or was suffering from some other cause. Jim Hardnuckle did not seem to be at all penitent for being the cause of the catastrophe which came so near terminating fatally, but rather felt disposed to joke about the matter.

"Well, old 'Sourkrout,'" said Jim, "I reckon you was water-logged for the first time in your life, but no one can say you was lagered."

This pun occasioned a general laugh.

"Bad cess to yez, Jim," said Patrick O'Gull, "why can't yez lave the exercisin' of them fists for the spalpeens what interfere wid 'lections by challengin' honest voters, and not be practizin' on yer friends?"

"I think," said Jim, "I've done a real service to our Christian friend, the Dutchman; for I've showed him that he can git dead drunk on water, if he only drinks enough of it; and he says that he can't drink lager enough to make him tight. After this, when he's too fur from a brewery, and wants to get on a spree, all he has to do is to make a dive into the water, and wait for some big Newfoundland dog to come and pull him out."

"You bet," said another, "he never drinks as much water as that agin unless it's forced down his throat from the hose of a steam fire-engine."

"Mine Gott, mine frents," said the German, "de tog hab more bluck dan all yous but togetter, py tam!"

"The dog," said Jim, "didn't want you to spile the water that he has to drink."

"Yes, old Limburger," said another, "I'll warrant you've spiled all the water in this pond. Don't you hear them geese swearin' at you for 'pregnatin' their drink with villainous lager and Limburger cheese? I s'pose you can understand them, for they say goose-talk and Dutch is all the same thing."

"You not know so mugch as von tam goose himself. To save a frent from trown, you not py stan."

"Oh! now, don't say you nix-fy-stan the geese. That's too thin."

"Mine Gott, vot a fool! I zay you not py stan to save von frent from trown in de trink—de vater."

"Oh! he says he wants to go to town to git a drink

of water. Why don't you take a swig from the pond? You'll find it's both victuals and drink; for it's a mixture of sourkrout, Limburger and lager."

"Oh! my, shall I pust mit mad at von pig fool!"

"Well, I declare! now he wants to go on a· bust like mad, and get big and full. I thought he got full enough, and come near enough to bustin' with water."

"Mine Gott! save me from prake his head. For von shtone I shtoop."

"If soup is what you want, the pond is the place to get it. It's good sourkrout and Limburger soup. Take a drink of it."

"You pe von idyut. You stays here and trinks de vater you ligs. I koes to de house and trinks te prandy."

Saying this, the German gathered himself up, and trudged away in high disdain, and he was soon followed by all the company except Horace and Mr. Graphic. After the gang had gotten out of hearing, Horace said:

"I am somewhat astonished, Mr. Graphic, to find a gentleman of your appearance and tone domiciled with such a crew as those who have just taken their disagreeable presence from us."

"My friend," said Mr. Graphic, "I am an artist pursuing my vocation in sketching with brush and pencil here in the mountains. I not only have splendid natural subjects here, but also find these people an exciting study. I don't know where a man of my profession could find a more pregnant locality."

"I have," said Horace, "heard of the operations of this Club before, but was not aware that they had any such den in the mountains as this; nor that their connections were as extensive, and embrace so many classes of the community as represented by that double-distilled essence of snobbery, Mr. Sindandy."

"While there is no especial effort made," said Mr. Graphic, "to keep the existence of this Club House a secret, there is no effort made to advertise its whereabouts; and owing to its obscure position, it is comparatively little known."

"Well, Mr. Graphic," said Horace, "I have observed the corruption of mankind till I have about lost all faith in human nature. About two years ago I left my native village, and repaired to a large city to practice my profession. This summer I came out here to spend a couple of months, thinking that a sojourn among the honest mountaineers would refresh me, and give me renewed faith in man. But what is the first discovery I make? Why, that there is an organized system of corruption in the country worse than I ever dreamed of. And that the very men who are engaged in it, instead of making it a secret, flaunt it in your face as if it were something meritorious rather than infamous. The fact that these men talk of their iniquities so openly, rather leads me to suspect that I have fallen among a lot of lunatics, who are affected with the hallucination that they are governing the State, and that all they have said are but the unreal vagaries of insanity; for it would certainly seem that men to be successful in such iniquities must necessarily be more secret about their mode of operations."

"What you have heard here," said Mr. Graphic, "is but too true; and the actors in this drama are at least sane enough to fasten themselves like leeches on the public treasury, from which they draw the funds which support their enormous extravagance. Their operations and connections are too extended to admit of secrecy. Any attempt to keep their matters from the public would surely be attended with exposure, for some one would certainly turn informer. Therefore they put on a bold front, and as nobody is under the bond of secrecy, no one has any particular object to go into exposures. Doubtless, many members of the Club regard their proceedings as perfectly right and proper, for the very reason that they are done so openly. Such a brainless fellow as that Sindandy is of much more value to the Club than a man of greater ability; for he apparently has not sense enough to distinguish between right and wrong, and he will talk of the most infamous public robberies with all the *naivete* of one who is relating some meritorious, religious enterprise in which he is engaged. Such stupendous innocence deceives more people than you dream of into an acquiescence in the idea that the infamous practices that he speaks of with such unsophisticated simplicity, are probably entirely legitimate in public affairs. I hardly know what to think of the fellow; whether he is most knave or most fool."

"What do you think the world is coming to, Mr. Graphic," said Horace. "This deterioration of the human race is observable not only in public affairs, in which both political parties seem equally venal,—it pervades everything. It is to be seen in business, in church affairs, and in the family circle. If you employ a clerk in your store, you have to set up safeguards, to keep him from robbing you; if you are a stockholder in a bank, you are sleeping on a constant rack, in view of the probability that the cashier will embezzle the funds; if you have a competence, and invest it in real estate, you are troubled lest the rascality of public officials may leave the title imperfect. Every man apparently seems to be aiming to enrich himself by whatever means he may. No one seems to act on the assumption that his fellows will deal honestly by him from principle; and acting with this view, each seems determined to appropriate to his own use whatever comes in his way. Honesty is looked upon as lunacy. For instance, if a man through any transaction gets possession of a large amount of money which the law would allow him to keep, but which does not morally belong to him, and should he restore it to the proper owners simply on principle, he is looked upon either as a sentimental softhead, who desires to build up a vain reputation for honesty, or else as a positive lunatic, who does not possess the right kind of faculties for a successful business man. What is called the world, cannot appreciate any act of genuine honesty, regarding it either as the vagary of a crazy man, or the hypocrisy of one who has some ulterior design, intending to profit by it in some way in the future. People appear to have no moral regard for the right of property. Indeed, except as we are absolutely protected by the letter of the law, we might as well have relapsed into barbarism; for men will appropriate to their own use everything they can; the only question arising in their minds is, not, 'Does this rightfully belong to me?' but, 'Can I hold it?'

"As regards property, the custom governing men seems to be a system of reprisals. A man loses to-day through the sharpness of an individual with whom he has dealings, who has some advantage of him, and takes it. To-morrow the loser sees an opportunity to make up his loss by a similar act of chicanery; and it matters not that it is not the same person who fleeced him. He can make up his loss by just such a trick as was practiced on himself, and he does it. There is little doing business on the principle that those with whom we have dealings, do right simply because it is right. Each one occupies his business position as if it were a fortress, and sets up his defences on every hand. If he leaves some salient point undefended, he expects some business assailant to storm that portion of his works, and capture a part of his funds. If he escapes such a misfortune, he attributes it not to the forbearance or honesty of the one who had the opportunity, but to his want of generalship. He is constantly on the alert not only to defend his own position, but to seek a favorable opportunity to make a sortie on some weak point of an antagonist. Not only must he watch those who would assail him from without; he must be constantly on the guard against treachery in his own garrison. Just as he considers the effects of other owners his own lawful plunder, provided he can get them in a *business* way, so his own employes are apt to look upon his funds as something on which they have the privilege of foraging. By his method of doing business he has taught them that the only test of ownership is possession under circumstances that will not render them liable to be dealt with at the hands of the law. The villainy their employer teaches them they execute, embezzling his funds as remorselessly as he takes those of his fellow business men by technically-legal means.

"Observe how men violate contracts when it no longer suits their purposes to fulfill them. See, when a contract is made, how provisions are piled upon provisions in order that there may be no loophole left for either party to creep out. The most solemn obligations have no weight whatever with men who think it to their interest to repudiate a contract; provided they can do it without injuring themselves. This idea is fully recognized in making contracts; and provisions are made by which it is intended that the party who recedes shall be thrown into an abyss or encounter a spring-gun, the discharge of which shall slaughter him. We might say that the rule governing the making of contracts, is to drive full of sharp spikes the only road over which parties have a chance to retreat, that they may be impaled in case they attempt to repudiate their obligations. Whoever, in making a contract, neglects to dig a pit, to set a spring-gun, to obstruct the retrograde path with *chevaux-de-frise*, to destroy the person who would repudiate it, only incurs the derision of his neighbors in case the compact is broken to his disadvantage.

"What a glorious world this would be if men could agree to deal with each other without this complication of chicanery. And they would be just as well off pecuniarily in the end, and infinitely better morally. The energies they expend in trying to over-reach each other, could be devoted to the legimate improvement of their fortunes. The material they use in fortifying themselves against the rascalities which they infer their neighbors will commit upon them, because they practice just such things themselves, might be saved. There certainly would then be a greater amount of material produced; and consequently there would be more wealth in the country for men to accumulate. It could be gotten honestly with less labor than is now expended to get it dishonestly. Employes, observing a high moral tone among capitalists and owners, would fall into habits of honesty, and there would be fewer defalcations.

"But the demoralization observable in the business and political world, finds a counterpart in the social and religious community. Wives have proved false to their husbands, and husbands to their wives, to such an extent that one may be led to doubt whether there is any longer any virtue left in either sex. Religious societies have become impure; and I can hardly see what the whole world taken together amounts to, except it be a raging, seething, putrid caldron of perdition."

Horace ceased, apparently exhausted with the workings of an agonized spirit, and Mr. Graphic said:

"Ah! my friend, what you say is true with certain restrictions; but you do not take a healthy view of matters. Things are by no means so bad as you picture them.

Look about you, and you will see that even this corrupt Leech Club, who now, in a great measure, control public affairs, find in Society a check on their iniquities; for they dare not proceed beyond a certain limit."

Horace made no reply to this, apparently having no desire to pursue the subject further, and closed by saying:

"Well, I came out here in the mountains to escape for a while the influence of the vortex of corruption, and am like the man who came down from Jerusalem to Jericho, and fell among thieves. I think you will prove to be my good Samaritan. I have been invited to become an inmate of this establishment for a time, and as there seems to be no escaping from the city of destruction, I might as well stop here as anywhere. I shall at least have an opportunity here of seeing how bad the very worst phase of mankind is; for I take it that none worse can be found, not even in the penitentiary."

CHAPTER VII.

A MIXED PARTY.

The "castle" of the Leech Club was situated some three or four miles from the nearest settlements of the rural population in that region. The members of the Club had made some acquaintances among the natives. Considerable of their supplies were obtained in the neighborhood, and the people of the vicinity frequently visited the Club House to dispose of their chickens, eggs, vegetables and other articles for immediate use. The general impression prevailed among the country people that the Club House was simply the residence of some city folks, who located in that out-of-the-way place in order that they might have a quiet and cool retreat for spending the summer months. A very rough and obscure road led to the settlements, and this was known only to those who had visited the Club House for the purpose of trafficking in rural produce, or had been invited there on some festive occasion. It must not be inferred that the native inhabitants were all farmers in moderate circumstances. There were a very few men of large wealth in the surrounding country, who had grown rich in the business of tanning leather. The tannery business was at one time a large interest in that section of country; though of late years it has greatly fallen into decay, owing to the exhaustion of the hemlock bark.

The native population are quite socially disposed, meeting frequently for enjoyment at "quiltings," "apple-cuts," and other frolicsome gatherings. There are generally two or three in every neighborhood who can saw the violin, and seldom is there a considerable company together but at least one or two fiddlers will be found among the number. Though the girls may have come together ostensibly to quilt, or both girls and young men may have assembled for the seeming purpose of peeling apples, the main object is that which most concerns all young people. Should a stranger peep in at the window, instead of seeing a lot of demure young women industriously plying their needles around a quilt, or a circle of both sexes peeling and slicing apples, he will more likely see a circle standing upon the floor with hands linked, surrounding a young man and woman in the centre of the ring, their voices joining in some such chorus as the following:

> Green grow the rushes, O,
> Green grow the rushes, O,
> Kiss her quick and let her go,
> Don't muss her ruffles, O.

Then if his acoustic organs are ordinarily acute, he will hear a smack that will remind him of anything but dried apples. One of the parties is released from durance, within the girdling ring, by the magic process of a kiss, and the circle renews its rotation, this time, perhaps, singing something like the following:

> Now the buckwheat's in the barn,
> The best produce grows on the farm;
> Now's the time for you to choose;
> Now's the time to win or lose;
> To get the mitten is no disgrace,
> For oftentimes it's been the case.

If you were where you could hear, but not see, the performance, you might infer that the young fellow had gotten the mitten, and in a rage had attempted to fire off a pistol at some one; for you can plainly hear a noise like the explosion of a percussion cap. But don't be alarmed; the lady smiles, and the gentleman looks as though he would like to receive a pair of such mittens as that. Again the circle moves on, and you hear the following in lively chorus:

> Ripest apples soon are rotten,
> Hottest love is soonest cold;
> Young men's vows are soon forgotten,—
> Pray, pretty maid, don't be too bold.

You immediately declare to yourself that it is no rotten apple that you hear some young man smack his lips over; and that notwithstanding the caution to the pretty maid not to "be too bold," she did not hesitate to put the tempting fruit to his lips.

Keeping your place a while longer in this pardonable evesdropping, you will hear the tum, tum, tum, of the violin, as the fiddler touches its strings, tuning it for the dance. Pretty soon you hear the "honors all," of the musician, and the scraping of the dancers as they bow to each other. Then commence the sweet tones of the violin, and the musician sings out in a clear, distinct voice: "Tops right and left," and you hear the pit-pat of the dancers' feet, and you know that they are sailing forward and backward in the exhilarating saltation.

Not the least pleasant part of the performance is the closing of the party, when the young men "go home with the girls." With only the owls and the katy-dids to witness the rapturous words of the swains, it may be inferred that there are many things said not intended for the ear of the reader. He may ask the nocturnal witnesses, but his only satisfaction from the owl will be the Yankee response of asking another question: "Who? who? who?" while the insects on the trees will give him such contradictory information as: "Katy-did, Katy-did; Katy-didn't, Katy-didn't; Katy-did, Katy-didn't; Katy-did; Katy-didn't; Katy-did, she-did; Katy-didn't, she-didn't; I-say-she-did, I-say-she-did; I-say-she-didn't, I-say-she-didn't; she-did; she-didn't."

The reader will be but little the wiser from anything he may learn from the taciturn owl, or the disputacious katy-dids. If he wants to know whether Katy, or Mary or any of the other girls *did* consent to the proposals of their accompanying swains, he must observe the crop of weddings which the parson reaps, when "the buckwheat's in the barn."

Such are the innocent amusements of the people in that rural region. The day following one of these social gatherings, finds the young men back in the fields, attending to the crops, or "logging" on the new clearing, or in the barn swinging the flail; while the girls, who do not shirk all the cares of the household upon their mothers, are engaged in their domestic affairs, milking the cows, or making the spinning-wheel hum to supply yarn for the warm stockings and mittens for the coming winter—for the young ladies know how to give *mittens* that are pleasant to the young men, as well as some that are not.

The Leech Club delighted in astonishing the natives with a splendid entertainment. Not long after Horace had become domiciled in the establishment, preparations were made for a grand party. As the number present would probably exceed the capacity of the building, a pavilion was erected on a glade near the house. A floor was laid for dancing, and canvas was spread to keep off the night dews. An elevated platform was erected about midway of the pavilion, on one side, for the musicians.

Everything being in readiness, the country people who were invited, began to assemble early in the afternoon; for it would be dangerous traveling the mountain trail which led to the Club House in the night. They came in lumbering conveyances, such as could best travel the mountain roads; some on horseback; while others having left their teams in good care at a point where the way became most difficult, trudged the remainder of the distance on foot. Miss Shoeman, the rich tanner's daughter, and Miss Greenwood, the daughter of the rich lumberman, came together on a sort of "buckboard," drawn by a span of horses driven by an experienced mountaineer.

As the clumsy vehicle trundled over the rough trail, the young ladies danced up and down in their seat at a rate that would have put to the test the stays of tight-laced city belles. But they did not seem to mind this tossing about in the least, their rosy cheeks showing that they were inured to the rough usage of the mountain roads. On arriving at the Club House, all were provided with refreshments and comfortable quarters till evening, when the festivities were to begin.

The tall peaks around threw their giant shadows down upon the landscape; the sun retreated slowly below the western horizon, saluting the salient crests of the mountains with a radiant, farewell kiss, as he bid them good-night; and then the goddess of slumber advanced and threw her mantle over the scene, and the sombre hills around wore the appearance of repose. Now there was a blast of trumpets at the pavilion, and soon there was a swarming of people in the spacious bower, as of the gathering of many clans. They came forth from the Club House and its piazzas, and from many a cozy nook about the grounds, where they had been reposing for several hours, to join in the revelry of the evening. The gentlemen gave their arms to the ladies, and the first thing was a grand promenade up and down the pavilion.

This afforded a good opportunity for an observer to survey the company. It was a motley and heterogeneous assemblage. There were the gentlemen and ladies of the Leech Club dressed in the very gorgeousness of extravagance. Some of the gentlemen wore white pants and vests, with dark coats; others sported a dress in which the prevailing color was dark; while some were dressed chiefly in light-colored stuff—all of the richest material. Their hair and whiskers were dressed in the most elaborate manner, presenting every phase of hirsute fashion. The wearing of the mustache predominated. All these gentlemen fairly sparkled with jewelry and diamonds. There was no spot on their persons where there could be a reasonable excuse for putting some rich jewel or golden ornament, but had it.

And the ladies of the Leech Club surpassed the gentlemen thereof in richness of attire, for the reason that the ingenuity of the fair sex has invented more methods of heaping extraneous treasures upon their persons than men have ever yet been able to devise for loading theirs. Doubtless many ladies who have the means of gratifying this innate desire for display, have often lamented that they have not the strength of camels, to carry several hundred pounds of ornaments. If the moral worth of these Leech Club ladies had compared favorably with the pecuniary cost of their diamonds and attire, their price would have been incalculable. With their long trailing dresses, and their immense head-gear of chignons and false curls, they cut a majestic figure as they promenaded down the pavilion, hanging upon the arms of their gallants. One of the peculiarities of the fashions of this period is the excrescence of flummery attached to the back of a lady's dress just below the waist, giving it much the appearance of a hump on a camel's back.

The dress of the country people was in striking contrast with the gaudy attire of this new-fledged aristocracy from the city. The young men from the rural settlements, it is true, had on their holiday raiment; but this bore no more comparison to that of their city competitors than does the plumage of the useful, domesticated birds of the farm-yard, to that of the strutting peacock. Instead of the bejeweled, padded, laced figures of the city dandies, the country swains presented themselves in decent, but plain and often uncouth apparel, with very little attempt at ornamentation. The contrast between the city and country girls was still more marked than that between the males of the two localities. Instead of the rich, trailing robes of their city sisters, the country girls generally wore dresses in which they could walk without being in the least incommoded; and as few of them wore a great superfluity of skirts or hoops to give them a rounded appearance, their dresses hung about their persons, giving them a lank appearance; which was doubtless becoming enough in their own native fields or rustic residences, but which caused them to look like posts draped in female apparel, as compared to the walking dry-goods establishments from the city.

The promenade had continued for some time, when the musicians changed to a waltz, and the dancing commenced without further notice. It was much as if a whirlwind had made a raid upon a laundry, snatched up all sorts of garments, including those which had been stiffened by starch, and those which were still in a limpsy condition, the commonest kinds, and the richest, indiscriminately, and set the whole into an incongruous whirl; dancing up and down, commingling in an inconceivable mixture, now moving horizontally in a body as if by some common impulse, then again rotating, then moving laterally, through and through each other, like several charging battalions which had been thrown into confusion, then separating again and joining in one furious whirl, as if actuated with a new impulse by a blast from the lungs of Boreas— till the eye grew weary of trying to discover any method in the medley. This continued till the dancers were out of breath, when they drew off to the side seats, to rest. The next dance was a quadrille, in which the country dancers were more at home.

During the evening, Mr. Sindandy made himself very agreeable to Miss Shoeman, the rich tanner's daughter; and in doing so, by no means advanced his interests in the friendship of John Woodman, who appeared to regard it as his privilege to wait upon that young lady on this occasion. Persons unacquainted with the customs of society in certain rural districts, would find it difficult to comprehend the relations between John Woodman and Miss Shoeman. Woodman was poor, being the possessor only of a small clearing, from which he had to support a widowed mother. He was much esteemed for his correct and industrious habits, much given to reading, and better informed than most of his neighbors; and Miss Shoeman regarded him with a certain degree of favor. Though her father had become a millionaire through the profits of the tanning business, he had once been as poor as John Woodman. Still, such great wealth generally begets pride, and while he looked upon John as a very respectable young man, he did not by any means regard him as a proper match for his daughter. But Mr. Shoeman, notwithstanding his wealth, retained many of his old habits of living on a sort of equality with his poorer neighbors. This was the more natural, as there were few others in the section where he lived for him to associate with, and his family would have been nearly isolated from all social intercourse, had they not associated with those who were poor as they were once themselves. As there were no rich young men in the vicinity, it will therefore readily be seen why Miss Shoeman accepted a certain degree of attentions from John Woodman. Her father did not object to this state of things; but there was doubtless a tacit understanding between him and his daughter that there was a certain limit beyond which these attentions must not proceed. It is not improbable that Miss Shoeman had a deeper regard for John than she would have been willing to admit; for young ladies are not, like their more calculating parents, entirely guided in such matters by considerations of wealth and expediency.

The members of the Leech Club always had an eye to the main chance, and never let an opportunity slip to form an alliance that might add to their material wealth, and extend their political influence. Miss Shoeman was an only child, the heir to a large fortune; and her father was a man of considerable influence in his own county. This fact was known to Mr. Sindandy, and he determined to make the most of his opportunities. She danced with John Woodman in the first quadrille, but in the next Mr. Sindandy secured her for a partner. During the intervals in the dance, he was constantly pouring his twaddle into her ear; and this, with the flashing splendor of the dress of the swell, took amazingly with the unsophisticated country girl. The large wealth of her father, aside from a few solid home comforts, was chiefly invested in profitable real estate and bonds; on which he drew a semi-yearly interest, again to be profitably invested. She, therefore, had never before seen such splendid toilets, such magnificently-dressed gentlemen, except in one or two instances when she had visited places of amusement in the distant city, and then she had not been brought face to face with them, as on the present occasion.

"Oh! dear me, Mr. Sindandy," said Mary Shoeman, as, in the dance, one of the comet-tailed young ladies' dresses whirled up against her, almost carrying her off her feet, "if I should wear such a thing as that on my dress, I could hardly walk around, much less dance."

"Aw! Miss Shoeman," said Mr. Sindandy, "a young lady of youah beauty, gifts and wealth, should not spend her time entirely in the country, whea she has no opportunity to lea'n the accomplishments and usages of good society. With a little practice you would soon become as accomplished as any young lady you see hea."

"But," said Mary, "what do you suppose father would say to see me with such a kite's tail as that to my dress? Why, he'd ask me if that was a bob-sled I was dragging after me, to draw bark on."

"Youah fathah, Miss Shoeman, ought to take pride in seeing his daughtah dressed and accomplished as becomes her position. If you would spend the coming wintah in the city with my friend, Mrs. Grandola, I think you would nevah regret it. She is a lady of great cultivation and refinement, and undah her instructions you would profit greatly."

"My goodness," said Mary, her face brightening up as if with anticipation, "do you suppose I could ever learn to carry so much finery about with me as these young ladies do without being tripped up with it at every step?"

"Cehtainly, Miss Shoeman. I dah say that you can do many things which these young ladies cannot, which are much ha'dah to learn."

"Oh! yes," said Mary, "I don't suppose that one of them could milk a cow, or spin yarn."

By this time it became the turn of Mr. Sindandy and Miss Shoeman to lead off in the dance, while John Woodman and Phebe Greenwood, who were dancing on the sides in the same quadrille, came to a halt.

"What do you think of this company, Phebe?" said John. (Country people are not always particular to address a young lady as Miss.)

"To tell the truth, John, I don't think much of them. But I'm so bewildered that I hardly know what to think. What's your opinion, John?"

"I think that Mr. Sindandy, there, will some day reach a high position."

"How, a high position, John?"

"I think he's bound to be elevated by the hangman."

"Oh! John, I see what's the matter: you're jealous because he's dancing with Mary Shoeman."

"I think better of Mary," said John, "than to believe that she could be taken up with such a brainless dandy."

"John," said Phebe, "do you know how I feel in this crowd? I feel just as though I was in a den of robbers such as I have read about in story books; who live in the grandest manner on what they get by robbery."

"I guess you are not far wrong," said John, "judging from an account I heard Mr. Sindandy give of his gang, which he calls the Leech Club."

"What, John, you don't really mean to say that we are among a gang of robbers away off here in the mountains?"

"Not exactly in the sense that you mean, but robbers after all; but I don't mean that we are in any personal danger."

Phebe seemed to be reassured by this statement, though she instinctively nestled closer to John. And now they dashed off in the dance, and their conversation ended for the present.

As soon as the quadrille was finished, Mr. Sindandy managed to introduce Miss Shoeman to Mrs. Grandola, having previously given that excellent lady the cue in regard to what he wished her to say to the country girl.

"My dear," said Mrs. Grandola, "I am charmed with you. If I could only have you in the city with me for a month or two, with an occasional hint from me, you would become as accomplished and fascinating as any young lady you see here. The stuff is in you, and you only lack opportunity to develop your powers."

If Miss Shoeman had been a little better acquainted with the world, and been able to distinguish true culture and refinement from the most tawdry and vulgar display, she would have regarded the intimation that she might become as accomplished as the ignorant, besotted throng before her, as anything but a compliment. But the glare of diamonds and jewelry and the sea of rich robes, overpowered her understanding; and had an ape, or a gorilla, or an orang-outang, or even a donkey, appeared upon the scene dressed in the exquisite style of the males of the Leech Club, or the trailing flummery of the females thereof, she would have taken it for granted that the ornamented monstrosity was a fine gentleman or lady. She would have waltzed with Satan himself, had his cloven hoof been ornamented with such a splendid slipper as that of Mr. Sindandy, and his horns hooped with diamond rings such as glittered on that exquisite's fingers, and never would she have suspected that the Evil One was other than a member of the Club in good standing. Mary flushed up with evident pleasure at the compliments of Mrs. Grandola, and said:

"I would dearly like to learn something of city life with you, if father could spare me for awhile. I think I could then go back home and teach our homespun neighbors a little refinement."

"To be sure you could, my dear," said Mrs. Grandola. "You could return and be the reigning belle of the whole county. And what splendid entertainments you could give; and you could always have a number of brilliant stars from the city at your parties; for you would soon form an extensive acquaintance. And it would add amazingly to the influence of your family. A man of your father's wealth, my dear, ought to be a member of Congress; and who knows but he might be Governor of the State, if he would only use the means at his disposal. Many a man has become prominent in politics through the agency of a beautiful and accomplished daughter. And then," Mrs. Grandola added in a lower tone, "such a splendid husband as you might get, my dear. What would you say to Mr. Sindandy?

Mary blushed diffidently, as if to say, "Oh! dear, I could not expect to look as high as that."

There was one person in the company who evidently did not enjoy himself. Mr. Flitaway had protested from the first against building the pavilion outside of the charmed circle of the streams of water which surrounded the Club House, saying that the company would surely be disturbed by the ghosts of the Catskills. At first Mr. Flitaway joined in the festivities; but after a while he declared in an undertone to some of his intimate friends, that he occasionally saw a hideous looking object, who was evidently not among the invited guests, glide almost imperceptibly into the pavilion when a waltz was in progress, while the dancers were too much engaged to notice the apparition, waltz across the floor among the crowd, pass out of the pavilion on the other side, and disappear. Horace Lackfathe, who danced but little, was generally observing the dancers from a side seat, and Mr. Flitaway went and sat beside him. Mr. Flitaway told his story to Horace, but the latter rather expressed the opinion that it was some sort of optical delusion. The apparition did not seem to trouble any one but Mr. Flitaway, and therefore he could make no one believe that he saw anything unusual. Finally, however, he was able to point it out to Horace as it went almost like a flash across the floor among the waltzers. It had only appeared, according to Mr. Flitaway, during a waltz, when a sort of confusion prevailed, and it would not be so apt to attract attention. Whatever it was, it seemed to take especial pains to show itself to Mr. Flitaway. Horace observed that, in passing out of the pavilion, it caused the boughs which formed the sides of the bower to part, and he thought he heard a rustling among the bushes, as of some one running away. A feeling of relief came over him; for he reasoned that a ghost could make no impression on material objects, not even on so slight a substance as a green bough; therefore the strange object must be a creature of flesh and blood. This sort of reasoning, however, does not comport with the spiritual stories that have become common in these latter days.

It was drawing toward the time for supper; and the last dance before sitting down to the sumptuous refreshments was to be a Virginia reel. Two long lines of dancers were formed the whole length of the pavilion, the ladies in one line, the gentlemen in the other, the two facing each other. The incongruous elements of the company were here brought together in contrasts and encounters that were calculated to excite the risibilities of an observer.

The music struck up, and first a young countryman in his homespun habit, and a city young lady in rich trailing robes, from opposite ends of the two confronting lines, went charging at each other like two skirmishers of separate hostile armies preparatory to the conflict, the main forces standing, and calmly viewing the procedure, as if to say, " our turn will soon come." The two skirmishers did not rush furiously at each other like the mail-clad knights of old, but came corveting, dancing, slowly, as if mounted on gay steeds, such as we have all seen proudly bearing militia officers in holiday uniform in a Fourth of July parade, prancing at the head of a procession. But if the two initiatory skirmishers came slowly, more terrible was the encounter when they met. Their mission was apparently simply to meet, cross swords, return and report to their respective forces. But the young lady in wheeling "about face," must necessarily impart an impetus to her train that would place it in the rear. In doing so, she gave it such a flop that it wound completely around the legs of the young man. Having thus his organs of locomotion in chancery, he was, as we might say, unhorsed, and brought flat on the floor; and as the lady now had an appendage to her train which was not placed there by the *modiste*, and much more than she was ever calculated to draw, was also, so to speak, floored, and both skirmishers were placed *hors de combat*. Other light troops rushed to the aid of the discomfited ones; the young man on being released from durance, was found to have suffered no serious wounds, nor the young lady either; but she had a much damaged trail.

This circumstance afforded considerable merriment among the country people, and such as were standing together so as to be able to converse without being overheard by their city friends, cracked a good many jokes on the contretemps.

"Jim," said one, " is good at startin' a deer from cover, but he got on the wrong trail that time."

" The trouble is," said another, " that Jim is more used to follerin' deer than foxes. He ain't up to all the twistins and turnin's of them sharp animals."

" That trail," said another, " is so completely wiped out, I don't believe a dog, or even an Injun, would think of follerin' it now."

" Don't be uneasy," said another, "there'll be enough that'll hunt up the game, even if the trail is lost."

" You think, then," said another, " that a fox is worth huntin' even after the hide is all torn off. Why, man, you can't eat 'em; I wouldn't give two cents for the animal without the fur."

"Oh! Bill," said the other, "that's rather too bad. Didn't you see how lovin'ly that city chap took her up. I don't doubt but he'd liked to took a taste of her; though as for the eatin', he might find her a tough morsel before he got through."

"Thinks I to myself," said the other, "when I seen that city gal hitch on to Jim with her ropes, you're in for it now, old boy. She's goin' to snake you along just like we haul a log out of the woods. But her ox-chain wasn't strong enough. Sich flimsy tacklin' may do to rope in one of them dandified city chaps, but you can't tow a country feller along with such weak gear."

"True as preachin'," said the other; "I reckon Jim would be towed along a good deal faster by Sallie Goodsel's calico apron strings, than the fudgery of that city miss."

Each party having carried off its wounded, sent each a new skirmisher prancing through the center, and this time, luck would have it, both were natives to the manner born, and accustomed to the mountain warfare. They danced down and back without any mishap, showing how much more effective provincial troops are for certain kinds of service than regulars. In our early Colonial times, the British General Braddock was defeated by ignoring his provincial allies.

A Virginia reel is one of the most exciting and amusing of country dances, when participated in by those who are unencumbered by a superfluity of dress to impede the maneuvering. After the mishap mentioned, the dance proceeded, the city girls certainly displaying commendable skill in engineering their trains, and keeping them from being smashed by the bipedal locomotives. But notwithstanding the vigilance of the fair engineers, there was occasionally a train telescoped and thrown from the track. The countrymen avoided the trails of the ladies as they would, when not armed with their trusty rifles, shun the trail of a panther in the forest.

The whole set had just completed the grand movement of marching and counter-marching, coming to a halt in two lines facing each other, as at the beginning;

when they were treated to an exhibition that struck the whole company with consternation. A hideous looking object, in appearance, part man, part demon, came spinning almost like a flash down between the two lines of dancers, so near that it almost brushed their clothing. The apparition brought with it a blast of air cold as from the icy caves of the mountains; described by those who felt it as striking a chill to their very bones. The faces of both men and women blanched with terror, and amid the wildest shrieks the dancers scattered from their places. The apparition in a twinkling passed out of the pavilion, and so great was the consternation of the company that pursuit was hardly thought of. The only one who retained his presence of mind was Horace Lackfathe. He had seen the apparition, whatever it was, before, and had been studying on it. With a speed only less than that of the nocturnal visitor he pursued. He at least discovered that it had not dissolved into thin air immediately on leaving the pavilion; for he saw it, by the dim light of the moon, making undiminished speed toward a perpendicular ledge of rocks. Urged on to superhuman exertions by the hope of discovering the key to this mystery, Horace flew like the wind after the retreating apparition. He gained on it; its speed appeared not to be so great as at first. How Horace went at such speed over such rocks, and through bushes without being tripped and bruised, he could never afterwards tell. In the furious excitement of the chase, he felt no exhaustion, nor looked upon the ground he trod. Had there been a deep abyss before him, he would have dashed into it, for his eye was fixed only on the fugitive figure. Now he can almost touch it, and he feels certain that it cannot escape him, for just before is an unbroken, impassable ledge of rocks. Straining every nerve, Horace's right hand grasps a revolver in his breast pocket, ready for an encounter should the fugitive show resistance. The sharp click of the lock, as Horace cocked the pistol, must have caused the nerves of the apparition to quake, provided it had any fears of leaden bullets. But Horace does not fire; he feels certain that his game will soon be driven to the wall, when he will capture it alive. He has for two or three minutes been on the point of grasping the fugitive, but always finds it just out of his reach. Now he throws all his force into a furious bound forward; he fairly flies, and catches the garments of the apparition— he has it—no, it is but some leaves from a bush that his hand comes in contact with. On, on, rush pursued and pursuer like shooting stars ricocheting over the sombre heath. And now the crisis is at hand. The perpendicular ledge of rocks is not ten feet off, and the apparition plunges into a thick clump of bushes at the base of the precipice. Horace rushes in without the least hesitation. The bushes would not more than afford cover for three persons, and surely Horace can have no difficulty in laying hands on the fugitive. He clutches around wildly among the bushes. He has embraced the whole space with his encircling arms, but with the exception of drawing the brambles to his breast, he might as well have clasped the empty air. He rakes the circumscribed space with the drag-net of his arms, and finds it like fishing in the Dead Sea. He obtains no food for the curiosity of his starving soul by dipping his net in such an unfruitful conservatory. Having satisfied himself that there was nothing in the bushes, and that there was no method of escaping through, or climbing the precipice, he stepped back a few paces. There on top of the ledge, out of his reach, sat the object of his pursuit.

"Man, ghost or devil," said Horace, aiming his revolver at the apparition, "stir not a peg, or the contents of these six chambers will verify whether you are proof against gunpowder and lead!"

"Presumptuous young man!" said the strange object, "you might as well discharge your weapon at the unsubstantial air. Be thankful that I have spared your life. Know you not that I might have led you to death twenty times during your mad pursuit. Had I turned a little from the course, you would have been led over a precipice and dashed to pieces. Return to your friends, and try not to pry into mysteries that are not for such as you to know."

"Who, and what are you," said Horace, " that prowls about in hideous masquerade, frightening the ignorant with your vain mummery? I will teach you a lesson that will be a warning to impostors. Now, come down from that perch and surrender yourself, or I will see what effect cold lead will have on your ghostly person."

"As for what I am, young man, it is enough that I am nothing that you can harm, or that wishes to harm you or yours."

"If you have no intention to do harm, why do you intrude in hideous attire into a festive company, frightening frail women into hysterics, and marring the pleasure of those who would enjoy themselves?"

"Ask the thunder, which in terrific volume, often reverberates through the recesses of these eternal rocks and hills, why it does not cease its rolling because, perchance, frail mortals will be frightened at the voice of supernal power! I am but fulfilling my destiny, and those who do not like my presence, must not invade my dominions, to practice a round of licentiousness as hateful to the powers of these secluded mountains as my own presence seems to be to those immoral revelers. I trouble no one who does not come to corrupt the ancient customs of these hills."

"You certainly seem to be a religious demon. You may consider it your duty to break up any party of pleasure that sees fit to visit what you are pleased to call your realm. But if you don't come down from there without further parley, I fire."

"Young man, I could in an instant summon a legion to my aid that would make you quail. But I spare you. Those whom I trouble are licentious invaders, whose cause I charge you not to embrace, if you are not one of their number."

"Once more, I say, come down from there as you went up, or I fire."

A hollow laugh, which the gorges and caverns of the mountains seemed to take up, and re-echo, till it appeared like rumbling thunder, was the only reply. This was followed by the quick report of Horace's pistol, three barrels being fired in quick succession. For an instant Horace was blinded by the smoke; the owls were startled from their roost, and set up a promiscuous hooting, while a hundred echoes from the rocks might have created the impression that the apparition had summoned a legion of his followers, each discharging a pistol at his assailant.

But as the smoke cleared away, Horace saw nothing but the bare rock where the strange being had sat. He was about to turn and depart, when his attention was attracted to another part of the ledge. There he saw the apparition standing. With a wave of the hand it exclaimed:

"Begone! begone! I spare you!" and immediately disappeared.

Horace now started to regain the Club House. He was confounded at the difficulty and danger of the way. He wondered how he had passed over the ground at such inconceivable speed, without falling into frightful chasms on every hand, and being dashed to pieces. He was struck with the recollection that the strange object had told him that it might have led him off precipices to his destruction. With careful climbing and feeling his way, he finally reached the house; strange to say, not having received a bruise or a scratch.

When Horace reached the pavilion, he found the company recovered from their fright. Some of the stronger minded men and women of the Leech Club try to sooth the excited nerves of the company by making light of the occurrence, expressing the belief that the apparition was nothing more than the wanton freak of some monomaniac dweller in the mountains. As Horace had not been missed from the company, he said nothing about his strange adventure, not desiring to excite the fears of the ladies. It was now about midnight, and the company was about to adjourn to the Club House for supper. This necessitated a brief walk in the open air, and many looked suspiciously around as they traversed the short distance between the pavilion and the Club House, as if they expected to see a goblin spring from under every bush. But if there were any such in the vicinity, they did not make their presence known, and nothing further occurred to disturb the excited nerves of the company.

Seated at tables glittering with costly plate, and loaded with choice viands, all apparently forgot the late unwelcome visitor in the discussion of the more substantial comforts set before them. There were disappearances almost as remarkable as that of the mysterious stranger; but no one seemed to be alarmed that such good things were constantly getting out of sight, nobody could say how. No one appeared to be frightened at the sight of even spirits disappearing with the more tangible and solid articles of the feast. It was quite evident that some were determined so thoroughly to familiarize themselves with spirits that no sudden apparition would hereafter frighten them. And as the feast progressed, and course succeeded course, and the sparkling wines flowed freely, the company became jovial, apparently caring so little for the presence of spectres that they were determined to leave but the ghost of what was on the tables and in the larder, and only the ghost of a chance for those who might be so unlucky as to come after them.

However fortified they were by the good cheer of the tables, no one proposed to go again into the pavilion; and plays and dances were commenced in the Club House, and kept up till the glow on the eastern mountain peaks told that the earth had completed half a revolution since the festivities had commenced, and that the sun would soon greet the rugged scene around with his morning salutation. Many had, however, at different times, retired to rest, and before day had fully broken, all had sought couches which had been improvised for the occasion, and all about the weird mansion was still.

It was middle of the forenoon before all had arisen, and partaken of the morning meal. After they had been duly refreshed, the country people prepared for their journey homeward. It was observed that John Woodman, who, on the arrival of the cavalcade at the Club House on the previous evening, had assisted Miss Shoeman from her rude vehicle, did not aid her in departing. Mr. Sindandy performed that office, and Mrs. Grandola was present, and with a superfluity of kisses and flattery, bade her good-bye. John Woodman, however, had the honor of waiting on Miss Greenwood, who rode with Miss Shoeman, notwithstanding the elegant Mr. Flitaway was anxious to tender his services. Miss Greenwood steadfastly ignored his advances, and accepted the proffered assistance of John.

The country people were now on the way to their homes, and the inhabitants of the castle were at liberty to comment as they liked on their rustic guests. So far as real, honest intelligence might be the criterion of judging between the two classes, the country people would have stood much the highest in the estimation of a philosophical observer; but if a knowledge of the ways of the world should be taken as the measure, then of course the city people would have been considered a little ahead.

After the country people had departed, they were the subjects of considerable comment among the inhabitants of the castle. There were angry strictures on their awkwardness, sneers at their want of breeding, and commiserations on their ignorance of the usages of *good society*. To hear these urbane people deprecate boorishness, a stranger who did not scrutinize their manners too closely, would never have supposed that most of them had come up from slums and cellars, to roll in redundant wealth.

CHAPTER VIII.

MR. SINDANDY AND MR. FLITAWAY RUSTICATE AMONG THE NATIVES.

The intimacy between John Woodman and Miss Shoeman was brought to a sudden termination. Not long after the party given by the Leech Club, John called at the house of the rich tanner, but was received so coolly by his daughter, that these visits were discontinued. There had never been anything more than a friendly intercourse between the young people; but this, under favorable circumstances, might have ripened into something warmer. How many such intimacies are there in every community where no promises have been made, no troth plighted, and yet one or the other or both of the parties considered it much more than a mere affair of ordinary friendship! The most exalted cases of love between the sexes are those in which a word on the subject has never been spoken, and which never reach the consummation of unity in marriage. The deepest pathos of the poets is found in those productions wherein the muse sings of affection unrequited, or that in which cruel destiny forever bars the union of the lovers. There is something so common-place about getting married that, though it is doubtless the *finale* devoutly to be wished for, it takes away a portion of the enchantment, the fruition, of love in which the parties have learned just not enough of each other to know that both are but human. It is said of pleasant dreams, that no person ever experienced the conclusion of one before awaking. He either awakes before completing the dream, or else it is turned off into some other channel before he reaches the delightful goal. It is so with day-dreams. Our pet theories, our visions of ambition, our well-laid plans for amassing wealth, our affairs of love, dissolve like the mirage of a dream as we approach their consummation. We find like children seeking the fabled silver spoon at the end of the rainbow, that the volatile splendor recedes as we chase it.

John Woodman did not appear to take to heart the cool treatment he received from Mary Shoeman. He had entertained for her a regard stronger than that of ordinary friendship; but the feeling had not taken deep enough root to cause him to repine when she rejected his attentions for one whom he despised as a strutting coxcomb. Mary had been completely dazed by the splendors of the Leech Club; and in her vain and inexperienced estimation, the tawdry men and women of that establishment appeared as the very paragons of gentility. Had Mary discarded John for one of his own fellows, one who had been brought up as he and she had in the rustic fashion of the country, he would have taken it more to heart. But he looked upon her favoring such a man as Sindandy as evidence that she lacked real worth, and was of a vain and fickle constitution. When we find some cherished fruit that we have been carefully preserving, eaten away by canker-worms and rotten at the core, we may indeed feel disappointed at our loss, but we no longer retain the corroding treasure in our choice casket. We throw it out to be appropriated by such as feed on garbage as their natural sustenance.

Moreover, John Woodman had found in Phebe Greenwood a more congenial *friend*. She held Mr. Sindandy and his clique in contempt at least as great as that in which they were regarded by John. It is astonishing how soon, under some circumstances, the Romeos find their Juliets. Having loved unavailingly, they come across a congenial spirit, and their affections are transferred with tenfold force to the new object. Nor is this an evidence of fickleness. As well say that a magnet is fickle because it no longer points to a substance which has freed itself of what little properties it had of attracting it. Few marry those for whom they first cherished a regard. Love is more an experiment than an instinct. Often young people imagine themselves in love, until some circumstance reveals the fact that their tastes and inclinations are totally at variance, and they gradually separate and gravitate toward those with whom they possess an affinity.

John Woodman had discovered that he and Phebe Greenwood at least agreed in despising the sham gentility and exaggerated display of the Leech Club; and thus they met on sympathetic ground. Whether their sympathies were to ripen into something more than friendship, time must show. Their conditions in regard to probable worldly possessions were as widely apart as those of John and Miss Shoeman, for Phebe Greenwood's father was also rich. He had, like Mr. Shoeman, commenced poor, and grown rich through a profitable trade in lumber. He had, like Mr. Shoeman, but slightly changed his method of living; and only those who knew him would have supposed that his circumstances were greatly different from those of his rural neighbors. His family associated with the surrounding community with as little restraint as if they only possessed an ordinary farm and a single saw-mill, instead of owning large tracts of land in two or three counties, and saw-mills on many streams.

Mr. Sindandy, Mr. Flitaway, Mrs. Grandola, and others of the Leech Club, had received an invitation from Mary Shoeman to visit her father's house. A couple of weeks after the grand party mentioned, the two gentlemen referred to, drove up in a buggy at the unpretending residence of Mr. Shoeman. They were cordially received by Mary, their horses cared for, and soon they were making themselves agreeable to the family in their own peculiar style. They were domiciled for a visit of several days; and as their earliest associations, before they profited by the beneficence of the Leech Club, were of a plainer nature than even the poorest of the rural population of that section, they found no trouble in making themselves at home at the rustic dwelling of the tanner. Though their present equipments, and dandified appearance, were as much out of place in that atmosphere as finely-dressed monkeys would be in the wilds of Africa, where such finery had never been imported, still they had known what it was in childhood to dine on cold victuals contributed from some hospitable kitchen. It may therefore be fairly inferred that they were subject to no great hardship in having to breakfast on fried pork, ham and eggs, with "warmed-up" potatoes, and coffee; to dine on pork and beans, green corn, apple dumplings, and pumpkin pies; the whole washed down by pure cold water from the spring, instead of sparkling wines; and to sup on mush and milk, bread and butter, sweetmeats, plain cake, and a cup of tea.

After they had been a couple of days at Mr. Shoeman's and had gotten on terms of intimacy with the family, Mr. Sindandy struck out in his own peculiar vein, edifying their rustic acquaintances with the high-toned ways of the world in which he and his companion moved. Mr. Flitaway said but little, apparently serving only as a sort of tender to Mr. Sindandy, always ready to confirm any statement made by that worthy.

"Aw! Mistah Shoeman," said the exquisite, "I wondah you don't emba'k in politics. A man of youah wealth and ability should at least control the county wheah he resides."

"I am on the wrong side," said Mr. Shoeman; "the party that I belong to is in the minority in this section of the country."

"I see," said Mr. Sindandy, "you don't know the ways of the political world. Why, sir, youah wealth would elect you on any ticket."

"Oh! no, sir," said Mr. Shoeman, "you mistake the independence of the country people. Although I give employment to hundreds of men, the most of them differ in politics with me, and they would not vote for me if I was running for office."

"Aw! Mistah Shoeman, you don't know all that men will do for a considahation."

"But, do you mean that I should resort to bribery to get into office?"

"By no means. Go around among the most influential men. Tell them that you would not think of such a thing as buying thea votes; that you know they don't diffah with you materially, and that you feel suah they will help you as a friend; that you want them to canvass around among thea friends for you, and that you know they cannot affoahd to spend their time for nothing. Tell them to draw on you for whatevah may be necessary to pay them for thea time. To some you will have to give fifty dollahs, some a hundred dollahs, and some, pe'haps, even as high as a thousand dollahs. Nevah feah but they will go right away to work for you for such good pay, and will no moah feel that they are bribed than if you should hiah them as traveling agents to sell youah leathah.

"The figures I named of fifty, a hundred and a thousand dollahs, are the highest you will have to pay. You can go around among the poorer class, and say to them also that you would not think of trying to buy thea votes, but that you know they will help you as a friend. Ask them to canvass a little for you among thea acquaintances, and say you know that they have families to suppoaht, and they cannot affoahd to lose thea time, and that you will give them five dollahs, ten dollahs, fifteen dollahs apiece, according to circumstances. Pretty soon you have got everybody to work for you, and no one is bribed.

"We membahs of the Leech Club always manage things without bribery. We nevah fail to get men to do what we want them to for a considahation, and we nevah bribed a man yet. We also get pay for ouah own honest labors in the Legislacha and elsewheah, and never accepted a bribe in ouah lives."

But for the unsophisticated audacity of Mr. Sindandy in laying down this remarkable code of political ethics, Mr. Shoeman would have immediately seen through the undisguised rascality of this method of manipulating an election. But Mr. Sindandy was such a pink of perfection—having gained the unqualified admiration of Miss Shoeman, and consequently of her mother—that Mr. Shoeman was actually wheedled into the blindness of his wife and daughter; who would have been astonished at nothing promulgated by the splendid, immaculate, infallible Sindandy; even had he told them that a common and legitimate amusement of his city friends was to set fire to a few blocks of houses, and, like Nero, keep time to the roaring conflagration by music and dancing. Mr. Shoeman remained silent for a little while, as if digesting the astonishment that had at first overpowered him at the thought that such practices could be right and proper, and then remarked:

"But, Mr. Sindandy, the method you speak of would cost an immense pile of money—many times what the office would be worth."

"Nevah feah for that," said the worthy expounder of ethics. "When you get to the Legislacha, you will find men who are willing to pay you to work for them, just as you have paid men to canvass for you; only they will pay you much highah. Why, it is nothing for a membah of the Legislacha to make ten thousand dollahs in a single day, and earn it too. Suppose you spend fifty, or a hundred thousand dollahs to be elected. I will guarantee that you shall have the money all back and moah besides, the first term you serve in the Legislacha."

Mr. Shoeman was utterly confounded at these statements. Could it be possible that such things were practiced, and that they were perfectly legitimate? It must be so, for the excellent, the elegant Mr. Sindandy, whom Mary and her mother regard as the paragon of refinement and morality, speaks of these practices with as little reservation as Mr. Shoeman would of a good operation in leather.

"And," continued Mr. Sindandy, "Mrs. Shoeman and her daughtah will have the benefit of residing part of the season at the Capital, which will be a great relief from the humdrum life of the country."

"Oh! yes, father, that would be so nice!" said Mary.

"And," said Mrs. Shoeman, "though I used to think we had a very pleasant home here, since I have heard

Mr. Sindandy tell about the fine things in the city, and how members of the Legislature are always called the Honorable Mr. So and So, and their wives the Honorable Mrs. So and So, I begin to think this a dull place, and want to see a little of the gay world. I'm sure we can afford it, and then Mr. Sindandy says we won't lose anything, but will rather make money by your going to the Legislature."

This was a clincher. Sindandy was the serpent that had entered that paradise, and Mrs. Shoeman was re-enacting the part of her ancestor, Eve. If Mr. Shoeman does not fall, he is not a true descendant of Adam.

Mr. Greenwood and Mr. Shoeman were neighbors, and there was considerable intercourse between the two families. In this manner Mr. Sindandy and Mr. Flitaway managed to get an introduction at Mr. Greenwood's. Mr. Flitaway exerted himself to obtain a footing there, but he received no encouragement from Phebe. Her father and mother, owing to the fact that he was endorsed by the Shoeman's, and doubtless a little taken by his splendid make-up, were disposed to look upon him with some degree of favor; and but for this fact, Phebe would hardly have treated him with civility. She preferred the companionship and good sense of John Woodman to the mincing flattery of the fop. Many was the rating which Phebe received from her friend, Mary Shoeman, for neglecting so favorable an opportunity to capture the splendid and wealthy city gentleman, and wasting her time with a penniless young man like John Woodman. Mary intimated that John might do well enough to help pass the time away when the neighborhood was not graced by a couple of elegant gentlemen, the likes of whom were seldom seen; but to let such a rare chance slip! How could Phebe be so preposterous?

Sindandy and Flitaway, during their stay in the country, took immense pleasure in astonishing the rustics. Dressed to the killing height of the fashions, glittering with diamonds and gems set in gold, they condescended to attend the rustic parties, to dance with the country girls in their plain calico dresses, and to shake the toil-hardened hands of the country swains. The two swells were the observed of all observers. The country girls were, many of them, as proud of dancing with the magnificent strangers as are some city belles to waltz with a prince of the royal blood, who may visit the new world. Nor is this said to their discredit. They had not seen such large quantities of the much-counterfeited coin called gentility, as to be able to detect the real from the spurious article. It is to be feared that some of them will learn too late that the glitter of highly polished brass is often greater than that of native gold, which has not undergone the refining process of the crucible.

We will now for a time leave Mr. Sindandy and Mr. Flitaway to their devices, while we return and see what is going on at the castle of the Leech Club.

CHAPTER IX.

THE HERMIT OF THE CATSKILLS.

Horace Lackfathe and Mr. Graphic were walking about the precincts of the castle one fine morning, when they fell in with an old resident, and native of the Catskill region, who had for some time been employed about the Leech Club establishment. Horace and his companion, naturally anxious to obtain information respecting this strange region, engaged in conversation with the old mountaineer. After some pumping, the old man saw that they were pleased to listen to him, and he became perfectly communicative. After relating various anecdotes, and describing many remarkable features of the mountains, he told them of a strange inhabitant, who made his home in the deep, dark gorges of the mountains; no one knew exactly where. Reduced to modern English the old man's story was as follows:

About three years ago there appeared in these mountains a man of middle age, dark skin, straight black hair, and features different from those of any race of men that the people here were accustomed to see. What was at first supposed to be a deformity of face, was finally decided to be the natural features of the aboriginal race, and the stranger was considered to be of Indian origin. No one had ever been able to discover his exact abiding place; but that such a person did live in the mountains was known from the fact that he had been met, and conversed with by hunters; who represented him as educated, and speaking good English. He invariably disappeared into the recesses of the mountains after holding the briefest interview with those who accidentally encountered him.

One story of his origin was that he was a descendant of the original Indian owners of the soil; that the remnant of his tribe had removed to the far West many years ago, and that he had returned to visit the graves of his ancestors. Some believed that he was the ghost of a great Indian, and that he had a whole tribe of aboriginal spirits at his command. Others who did not exactly accept the ghost story, still believed that he had a sort of connection with the goblins of the mountains, and that he could at any time bring them forth at his beck and call—that while he was in reality a being of flesh and blood, he was a sort of connecting link between the real and the unreal world. It was believed that he not only commanded the shadowy representatives of the red men who inhabited this region ages ago; but that the spirits of the more recently departed white men also recognized him as a leader. It was also believed that, though partaking of the nature of this world, having a physical form like other men, he still so far partook of the unsubstantial nature of his shadowy followers, that he could at any time vanish like the shadow of a cloud. The philosophy of those who held this theory, did not extend so deeply as to prompt them to explain what became of the physical frame of the dual being, when he dissolved into nothing.

As to the ability of the ghostly followers of this strange denizen to act on physical substance, there seemed to be a dispute. All apparently admitted that a spirit could not of itself move the slightest atom of matter, and consequently could not do the least personal harm to a human being. But many contended that the ghostly legion could act on matter through the physical agency of their human representative, the strange Hermit of the Catskills; that this mysterious individual, backed by his legion of goblins, possessed superhuman power to move from place to place like a flash; and that under such circumstances he was a match for a troop of mortals armed with the weapons of this world. It was, however, generally believed that he and his ghostly crew possessed no power to injure those who did not interfere with them in their wanderings through the mountain solitudes, or wantonly invade the deep, dark gorge where they held their habitation.

On hearing this curious story, Horace was immediately impressed with the idea that the subject of it must be one and the same as the apparition which had caused such consternation in the pavilion on the night of the party. Horace felt an irresistible desire to explore the mountains, and fathom this mystery. He could not prevail on the old mountaineer who related the story, to accompany him on such an exploring expedition. The latter would readily have joined him in a hunt, had the game been panthers or catamounts; but goblins were entirely out of his line. Nor could the old man give him any definite information respecting the residence of the dreaded Hermit, except that he had been most frequently seen in a certain deep, gloomy gorge; dark with the shades of gigantic trees; bounded by impassable precipices; strewn with a *debris* of boulders; with a boisterous stream of water running down the center. It was situated several miles from the castle.

A day or two afterwards Horace proposed to Mr. Graphic an excursion to the gorge mentioned as the probable residence of the strange hermit. Mr. Graphic was not possessed of the feverish anxiety of Horace to unravel the mysteries that had environed the castle; but he was not superstitious; and as the remarkable ravine mentioned, promised rare work for his brush and pencil, he readily consented to the expedition. With two or three days' provisions, two revolvers each, and a couple of blankets, they started for the Plutonian valley.

The old mountaineer who had given them the information, accompanied them for the first two or three miles, assisting in carrying their supplies. Then giving them directions for reaching the ravine, he returned; first having exhausted his eloquence to dissuade them from so presumptuous an undertaking. Parting from their guide, their way lay over trackless mountains. Clambering over rocks and fallen trees, scratched by underbrush, foot-sore from constant bruises received from the flinty pavement on which they trod, they pursued their wearisome way. Anon they would emerge upon an unwooded tract, where, some years before, fire had left but a desert of bare rocks, and black, scorched trunks of trees; where a vertical sun poured down his blistering rays on the weary travelers. It was indeed a relief to plunge into the timbered solitudes; even though greedy flies pounced upon them, to suck their blood when the sun no longer drew from them a torrent of perspiration.

Finally they reached a narrow defile, bounded on each side by a precipice. From this defile flowed a stream of water, beside which there was barely room to enter. This they knew from the description given by the old mountaineer, was the ravine they were seeking. Climbing from boulder to boulder, wet with the spray of the brawling stream, they make their way into the defile. As they proceed it widens, and soon they find themselves in a considerable valley, bounded on all sides by impassable walls of rock. And what an overpowering solitude! A thick growth of timber, pine, hemlock, and hardwood, so completely shuts out the light of the sun, that a semi-twilight prevails. Only here and there a few sickly rays find their way through chinks in the foliage; falling upon the rough carpet like the last faint smile of a dying sun, that was about to depart forever. Surely this must be the vale of Hades. Look which way they would, they were shut in by a precipice. Did the demon of the place wish to capture them, he had only to station one or two of his goblins to guard the outlet, and he had them. The *debris* of boulders strewn around, gave the surface the appearance of having been agitated by the subterranean action of a burning volcano underneath. No wonder that any one the least tainted with superstition should hesitate to enter this miniature Pandemonium. But for the constant brawling of the stream of water, the solitude would have been unendurable. For a time both Horace and Mr. Graphic seemed to be struck dumb by some unseen influence of this newly-found Tartarus. Mr. Graphic was the first to overcome the spell, remarking:

"Ah! Horace! verily we have entered the infernal regions. I felt, when we were passing through the defile, climbing, slipping, and sometimes wading through the stream, that we were really crossing the river Styx, and I thought of calling the ferryman Charon to our aid."

"Indeed," said Horace, "if we don't meet that Stygian boatman or some of his crew here, we need not seek them elsewhere, but may be content till they come for us of their own accord."

"Hark! what's that?" said Mr. Graphic.

"Nothing but the echo of our voices," said Horace. "Come, come, Mr. Graphic, you must not begin to be nervous so soon. Our researches have not commenced yet."

"Don't fear for me," said Mr. Graphic, as if ashamed of the surprise he had manifested. "If there is nothing more dangerous than ghosts here, I think we shall be able to manage them. The most I fear are panthers and catamounts; but with our well charged revolvers, and our trusty dog, I think we shall be able to manage them also."

"Hist! Did you see that?" This time the alarm came from Horace, and the dog growled. Mr. Graphic rallied Horace, but the latter exclaimed:

"The Lord preserve me, if I did not see a shadow dodge behind yonder rock!"

"Quite likely," said the other. "A gust of wind has parted the foliage of these dismal trees, and let in a little sunlight, which departing, caused a shadow."

"Such shadows," said Horace, "would not be likely to take human shape. Let us reconnoiter that rock, you taking the right and I the left flank."

"Nonsense! we are too tired just now to go chasing phantoms. Let us prepare our dinner. I believe there are trout in this stream. We will cut a couple of fishing rods, and throw the lines that we brought with us. What do you say to adding some of the speckled fish to our commissariat?"

"Good; we will throw our lines into this outlet of the lake of Tartarus, or the river Styx, whatever you please to call it; and we will have it understood that nothing shall divert us from our purpose until we shall have gotten our dinner—not even a ghost throwing his line from the opposite side of the stream, or Charon floating down the current in his ghastly boat!"

The two friends were soon trolling their hooks and lines over the swift water. And they were not mistaken in the surmise that the stream contained trout. The deep seclusion, and water kept constantly cold by the impenetrable shade, evidently rendered the stream the paradise of the delightful speckled fish. They took hold of the hooks with the readiness of unsophisticated gudgeons, which had not often been tempted to their destruction by the delusive bait. It was quite plain that the ghostly inhabitants of this dismal valley did not much indulge in the sport of fishing. The two anglers, charmed with the successful sport, continued it much longer than was necessary to supply their immediate wants, and ere they ceased, a couple dozen splendid trout were flopping about among the rocks where they were landed, their bright spots giving forth gleams of light, like sparks of sunshine in the gloom.

It was now past mid-day, and with appetites sharpened by their rough tramp, the successful anglers made haste to clean their fish, and prepare a fire to cook them. With a supply of butter, salt, bread and other necessaries, they soon sat down to a meal that the pampered guests of the best hotels in the country might have coveted. The honest and faithful dog, Tiger, was not neglected. Morsels as choice as any were constantly thrown to him. He lay off at a respectful distance, and as he, with great satisfaction, discussed the good fare with his masters, he apparently never forgot that they had embarked in an enterprise requiring constant vigilance. Anon the intelligent brute would elevate his ears, knit his brows, his countenance wearing the appearance of firm determination, but not malice, as he glanced around into the gloomy forest.

The repast finished, the next thing was to prepare a secure lodging place, as a base of operations, whence ulterior movements could be made. An overhanging rock was found, under which they could stand nearly erect. It formed a sort of cranny, not only covered overhead, but inclosed on three sides by rock. It was a work of no very great labor to gather some heavy stones, and inclose the third side, leaving a door barely large enough to crawl in. With a hatchet which they had brought with them, they cut some stout pieces of wood, by which they could secure the sally port of their fortress on the inside. Gathering some hemlock boughs, they made a very comfortable bed, spreading the blankets upon the pliant evergreens. They thus prepared a sconce, not much larger than was needful for them to lie down in, but a pretty good defense against panthers and catamounts, if not against nocturnal goblins.

Depositing their supplies within their Lilliputian castle, they made a brief survey of the valley. It was not extensive, there being not more than twenty or thirty acres within its precipitous walls; and at no place did they discover a break which would afford ingress or egress, except the point at which they entered. But they had not time to make a complete survey, for the sun was sinking behind the lofty peaks, and darkness set in before sunset. They returned to their fortress, and got up a lunch from the remains of their dinner. They then prepared a torch from materials which they had brought with them, to be used in case of an emergency, and, with the dog, retired within the portals of their castle, secured the door, and stretched themselves out on their rude couch for a night's rest. The dog lay at their feet, near the door, and they felt secure in the thought that the watchful animal would give the alarm in case of the approach of danger. As they lay at ease in their cozy retreat, they conversed in a low tone on the subject of their visit to this secluded vale.

"Do you know," said Mr. Graphic, "what I have thought about the strange, and apparently supernatural, manifestations that are prevalent in these mountains? I have frequently surmised that the Leech Club have something to do with them. I have thought that the apparitions are somehow gotten up to order by them, to keep intruders from frequenting this part of the country. My only fear in this investigation of ours is that we may find ourselves dealing with something more substantial than ghosts. What if it should turn out that that conclave of public thieves keep a den of outlaws in this very glen, to do their bidding, and to take care of such persons as may be dangerous to their plans of public plunder? They may have a secret cavern here in the mountains, as well for a retreat for themselves, as for a cover under which to dispose of such as may incur their vengance, either by the knife of the cut-throat or by a forced imprisonment in a cavern-cell. Should we meet with a gang of such gentry, we would hardly find ourselves numerous enough for the occasion."

"I have thought the same thing," said Horace, "but the evidence that the members of the Leech Club have an undoubted dread of these apparitions has convinced me that they are as much puzzled by them as we are. Still, I think they are rather glad of the presence of these mysterious appearances, as they have the effect of keeping away intruders, and the Club feel secure in their castle against any marauders. If the Club really have a gang of outlaws here in the mountains to perform dark deeds, I feel certain there are also another class of mysterious beings here, which have no connection with the Club; and the latter are as ignorant of their origin, nature and purposes as we are."

"You have," said Mr. Graphic, "heard the story of the discovery of gold in these mountains by the Dutch while they held the country; how the Dutch Governor Kieft sent an agent to Holland with a quantity of the ore, and the ship on which he sailed was lost, and all on board perished. Kieft himself, being succeeded in office by Stuyvesant, sailed for Holland with a quantity of the ore; but his ship was also lost, and with him was buried the knowledge of the whereabouts of the precious ore. From that day to this no one has been able again to discover it. Perhaps the mysterious beings lately appearing in these mountains have discovered the valuable secret, and wish to keep all others away."

Mr. Graphic did not say this because he thought it probable, but only gave it as one more theory; as men will do when investigating anything concerning which they are completely nonplused. So they continued to suggest theory after theory, none of which were in the least satisfactory to themselves, until their conversation died away into the slumbering sounds of the cricket and beetle, and they fell asleep; perchance to solve the mystery in dreams.

Nothing occurred to mar their slumbers till about midnight; when a medley of terror burst upon them, such as has seldom saluted the ears of mortals. Their courageous dog, with a howl, as if stricken with an overpowering fear, crawled up beside his masters. They were awakened by a medley of terrific sounds immediately around their habitation, which it was impossible to classify. It appeared to be a combination of the yell of the demon, the cry of the panther, the warwhoop of the Indian, and the wail of the damned. The awful sounds came from the forest, from the rock overhanging their habitation, and through every crevice of its walls; as if the fiends placed their mouths close up to the chinks to salute the horrified ears of the two devoted men with their demoniac yells. It verily appeared as if the two individuals were beset by a legion of goblins. Grasping their pistols, they crept up to the door, and endeavored to peer out through the chinks. All was as black as Tartarus. Not an object could be seen. For a moment they hesitated to light their torch, but soon concluded that, if they were beset by any real danger, their assailants would not long hesitate to make a more substantial attack on their fortress, and they would be better prepared to defend themselves in light than in darkness. The torch was accordingly lighted, and while Mr. Graphic opened a small port-hole, and thrust the light out into the thick darkness, Horace, pistol in hand, watched at another chink, ready to fire on anything that might be seen. The torch illuminated the gloomy trees and rocks, causing them to cast weird shadows, but not a semblance of a living being was to be seen. Still the noises continued, but from so many directions it was impossible to detect any particular spot as the lurking place of a member of the horrid crew. Sometimes the fearful sounds would die away entirely, and then start up again with tenfold terror. After watching for some time with torch protruding from the grotto, Horace saw a shadowy form flit athwart the beam of light, and instantly discharged his pistol at it. Though within point-blank range, and only a few feet off, the bullet had no effect on the apparition, and it glided away into the darkness. Then there followed another, and another, and another of the weird figures across the range of his revolver, at each one of which he discharged the weapon, until he emptied one pistol with as little effect as if he had fired at the empty air.

Whether owing to the discharge of the pistol, or whether the ghostly choir had become wearied with their infernal chorus, the unharmonious serenade soon ceased after the firing, having continued about half an hour. It would be impossible to describe the feelings of the two men as they once more breathed freely, and had time to collect their excited thoughts. Their grotto was a place of remarkable security, being protected overhead and on three sides by immovable rocks, and the third side, which was of small dimensions, was built up with heavy stones. They felt sure, with their four revolvers, they could defend themselves against twenty or thirty human assailants. Neither of them was superstitious, but what could they think when their bullets made no impression on these shadowy marauders? Men may be ever so stubborn in any belief, but when constant ocular demonstration is presented to them, apparently disproving their firm convictions, they begin to waver, and think they may be mistaken after all. The demonstration which appears to refute their previously strongly rooted belief, may be a delusion, still the repetition of it will shake their faith unless they can get to the bottom of it, and discover the fallacy. So the most absurd isms of the day find followers, if they can only keep up a specious system of deceptions until a considerable number of people grow into the belief that the plausible fallacies are real truths.

Hard knocks and blows will convince men of many things, when they have no means of meeting their adversaries with similar arguments; and the fearful blows just laid on the moral constitutions of Horace and his companion by the unearthly things which they had just witnessed, were working toward a change in their opinions respecting supernatural agencies.

They had drawn in their torch, fastened up the portholes, reloaded the discharged pistol, and taken means to make their grotto more secure than ever, and sat back in an easy position, apparently exhausted by the great strain their minds had undergone. The dog sat looking at them in a cowed, apologetic manner, as if to say: "You must excuse me, gentlemen, for the non-combative part I have acted in this matter. Show me a panther, a bear, a wolf, a catamount, or even a human enemy, and if old Tiger don't show himself foremost in the charge, then tie a stone to his neck, and throw him into yonder stream. But really, gentlemen, this is not in my line. I can't set these fangs into things impalpable. I can't throttle the wind, nor crush the heart and bowels of shadows without substance."

"This is fearful and wonderful," said Mr. Graphic, finally breaking the silence.

"Truly," said Horace, "those were no earthly sounds that we heard, nor earthly forms that I shot at; though I never admitted as much, even to myself, before."

"You are right; only the fiends of Hades could get up such an infernal discord. I verily believe that Pandemonium was emptied of its goblin legions, that they might give us an idea of hell's concerts."

"It, indeed, appeared as though a volcano had broken forth in this dread valley, which, instead of molten lava, sent forth an eruption of malignant spirits from the forgotten graves of many ages; and that Beelzebub, appearing in the midst, had organized an impromptu opera, set to the music of the Plutonian realms."

"Or, perchance, mischievous spirits have been playing on us a tremendous practical joke. You see they have left us unharmed, except the frightening we may have suffered." Mr. Graphic said this with a sort of venture at jesting, as if recovering from the freezing depression that the terrific exhibition had caused.

"And after all," said Horace, "this may be but the legerdemain of a few jugglers in pay of the Leech Club"—so slow are men to admit the truth of things they have made up their minds not to believe.

"Such a thing is possible," said Mr. Graphic. "Three or four persons gifted with the power of ventriloquism, might have created the hideous discord, and with the machinery of jugglers, might have caused the shadows which you shot at to flit before the beam of light radiating from our torch; but I find it as hard to believe that so much trouble could be taken to provide for such an exhibition in this out-of-the-way place, for the idle purpose of frightening two humble individuals like ourselves, as I do to believe that the affair was supernatural. I fear that this must ever remain one of those unexplained mysteries which have puzzled wise men from time immemorial. There certainly are many well authenticated cases in which the spirits of the dead have apparently revisited the earth and conferred with mortals. I do not mean to say that I positively believe this to be the case, but I do know that there are cases which can be explained in no other way."

"I shall," said Horace, "leave no stone unturned to fathom this mystery."

"And I," said Mr. Graphic, "believe that it is a duty we owe to mankind to get to the bottom of it. As men sacrifice themselves for a principle, or on the altar of science, I believe we are justified in periling even our lives to solve the problem here presented to us. Let us now to rest, to prepare ourselves for the beginning of a campaign to-morrow—it may be against evil-disposed men; it may be against fiends and goblins; but now that we are here, let us fight it out like valiant soldiers battling to know the truth."

With this they retired again to slumber. They were not again disturbed, but slept till the sun had shed as much light within the dreary valley as the matted foliage of the giant trees would permit.

When they issued forth upon the scene of the previous night's hideousness, revolver in hand, they looked carefully for any tracks of their disturbers. Not a sign of anything of the kind could be seen. The ground, littered with the usual fallen foliage of evergreens, bore no footprints of man or beast. It is true that living beings might have taken the pains to tread from rock to rock, and thus made no tracks; but this would have been a difficult operation in the night.

The sombre valley, though gloomy in the extreme, nevertheless possessed features of wild grandeur, which called forth the admiration of the artistic Mr. Graphic, and the naturally poetical Horace. The rugged, rocky precipices encircling it, the lofty and venerable trees, the turbulent stream thundering down in one almost continuous cascade through the center, rendered the solitary vale unique and enchanting beyond description. The two sojourners again threw their lines into the stream to catch the blithesome trout for their morning meal. Soon a number of the finny beauties were lifted from the foaming element, and were capering on the ground as if dancing the wild dance of the valley, to the music of the roaring waters. No one could grumble at the breakfast made at a fire kindled in the open air, with trout and articles from their haversacks, and water from the mountain stream. Tiger was encouraged to take his share, though he appeared half ashamed to come forward, as if he did not approve of his own conduct on the previous night.

Leaving their "traps" in their hut, with the door secured, and each armed with his two revolvers, they set out for a thorough exploration of the valley. Making a circuit around it, they found that the stream of water came down from the top of the cliff in a beautiful cascade at the head of the vale, and that it was increased by powerful springs within the valley. They learned to a certainty that there was no outlet to the glen except the one by which they entered. Having thus carefully examined the encircling precipices, they commenced searching every nook and cranny and rock in the vale. The dog had regained his courage and joined in the hunt.

They had continued this search several hours, without discovering aught of interest, when Horace felt certain he saw something dodge behind a distant rock. Without uttering the least note of alarm, he quietly communicated his suspicions to Mr. Graphic. The two agreed to move in different directions, and head off the skulker on two sides. The dog was well trained, and was kept close to Mr. Graphic. Stealthily they crept through the thick trees upon their intended prey. Finally they flank the rock, each at opposite sides, and behold, there stands a strange looking individual! On seeing the two intruders, he starts as if to retreat, but the two, with cocked pistols, spring forward and head him off. Thus he is hemmed in by the rock on one side, and two men armed to the teeth on the other. The assailants would not have been the least surprised had he vanished into nothing, but he did not. He halted; and in mutual silence assailants and assailed gazed on each other for about a minute. Finally Horace exclaimed:

"If my eyes don't deceive me, you are the wight that disturbed the party with ghostly masquerading, not long since. Now my good goblin, we will serve you as a certain man did an ass which dressed in a lion's skin to scare foolish people. We will strip off your masquerading garb, and show you to people in your true character."

The stranger said not a word, but Mr. Graphic detected a scornful smile play about his mouth.

"Come," said Horace, "take off that masquerading attire, and let us see what sort of a monster you are."

"More gently, Horace," said Mr. Graphic, "let us parley with him. I say, stranger, tell us who and what you are, whence you come, and whether you have aught to do with the seemingly infernal powers which haunt these mountains, and more especially this valley."

The stranger at first deigned no reply, and the expression of his countenance was that of ineffable scorn, as much as to say: "And who are you that expect me to answer all the vain questions that you see fit to propound?" Mr. Graphic observed this lofty bearing of the stranger, and his apparent indifference to the weapons leveled at him, and adopted a more conciliatory tone, as he said:

"My good sir, deign to tell us if you know aught of these mysteries. We have come here prompted by no idle curiosity. Our souls have been so greatly vexed by matters which we know not whether to class with the supernal or corporeal, that we could no longer contain ourselves without making an effort to unravel the dark problem. Then graciously say whether it is in your power to enlighten us. Whether mortal or spirit, if you have kindly feelings, let not our yearning souls starve and droop with ignorance! Give us such knowledge as you have, and whether it is what we seek or not, we shall be thankful."

"Do men asking favors," said the stranger, "do so

with weapons threatening those from whom they ask? You act rather like the highwayman, seeking what you demand at the muzzle of deadly fire-arms."

"True," said Mr. Graphic, "we have been sorely tried here, and looked upon any one we might meet as a probable enemy. This should serve as some palliation of our rudeness."

Here Mr. Graphic lowered his weapon, and Horace did likewise. As if recognizing their disposition to be civil, the stranger said:

"The few who know aught of me, call me the 'Hermit of the Catskills.' The remnant of my people removed from these hills far toward the setting sun, before my birth. I have come here to remain for a time to commune with the spirits of my ancestors. Who has a better right here than I?"

"Then," said Mr. Graphic, "you claim descent from the red men who inhabited these hills many scores of years ago."

"Yes."

"Tell us, pray, if you know anything of the wonderful and terrible manifestations that we have witnessed in this valley. Do you know whence came the awful sounds that last night saluted our ears, and the strange apparitions that flitted before our vision?"

"How shall I know," said the stranger, "what sounds men hear or what sights they see? All nature is full of sounds, apparitions, and mysteries. These mountains may be just now a favorite haunt of visitors from the spirit land. But there is nothing here but may be witnessed everywhere on a smaller scale. Think you the spirits of hundreds of generations never come back to their old haunts, or congregate in some favorite spot, to hold communion? I, as well as you, hear sounds; but I find them not terrible nor discordant. If you have heard the communications of another world, and been terrified thereby, it is because your earthly natures have not been able to comprehend the ways of those who have been released from the clogs of earth. Some mortals are so far favored, even on this sphere, as to be able to rise, in a measure, up to the standard of the eternal world."

"The whisperings from the myriads of spirits are

www.ingramcontent.com/pod-product-compliance
Lightning Source LLC
Chambersburg PA
CBHW020302090426
42735CB00009B/1183